THE BOOSEY & HAWKES MASTERWORKS LIBRARY

AARON COPLAND

BALLET MUSIC

MUSIQUE POUR LE BALLET
BALLETTMUSIK

Billy the Kid Suite

Four Dance Episodes from *Rodeo*

Appalachian Spring Suite (orchestral version)

London · New York · Berlin · Sydney

Publisher's note

The publishers have used their best efforts to clear the copyright for images used in this volume with the relevant owners and print suitable acknowledgements. If any copyright owner has not been consulted or an acknowledgement has been omitted, the publishers offer their apologies and will rectify the situation following formal notification.

Cover design by Lynette Williamson
Front cover picture: *The Southwest* by Walter Ufer (1876-1936)
Christie's Images, London/Bridgeman Art Library, London/New York

Printed and bound in England by Halstan & Co. Ltd, Amersham, Bucks.

Contents

COPLAND 2000

Preface

It was largely through his scores for the dance - both actual ballets and music referring to dance tunes and forms - that Aaron Copland found his distinctive voice and became one of the most representative American composers of the 20th century. While his three principal 'American' ballets - *Billy the Kid*, *Rodeo* and *Appalachian Spring* - were written in a comparatively short period between 1938 and 1944, his interest in the dance went back to the 1920s and persisted into the 1960s.

In 1922-24, while studying with Nadia Boulanger in Paris, he wrote a one-act ballet - his first orchestral work - entitled *Grohg*, based on Murnau's famous German horror film *Nosferatu*. It was never staged in Copland's lifetime, but from it he extracted the *Dance Symphony* with which he won his first major award, an RCA Victor recording prize, in 1929. Despite its German-expressionist background, the music of both ballet and symphony is infused with the young Copland's realization of the potential of jazz and blues. He explored these styles further in many later works, such as *Music for the Theater* (1925) with its 'Dance' and 'Burlesque' numbers and his second ballet, *Hear Ye! Hear Ye!* (1934). The latter was his first ballet on an American subject - a satirical courtroom drama featuring a trial for a nightclub murder, all in appropriate jazz style. *El salón México* (1936), inspired by a visit to a Mexico City dance-hall and containing actual Mexican folktunes, marks the entry of Latin-American folk-music into his personal idiom. Later scores in similar style are the *Danzón Cubano* (1942), an evocation of an indigenous Cuban dance, and the Mexican and Venezuelan dance-pieces which form the *Three Latin-American Sketches* (1959-71).

Thus when he came to write *Billy the Kid* in 1938 for Lincoln Kirstein's pioneering company Ballet Caravan, Copland was already expert in using folk material. He had looked to the Old West the year before, to provide material for his radio score *Prairie Journal*, and he was able to work several authentic cowboy songs into the new ballet (as well as some more Mexican material). This process continued in *Rodeo* (1942), written for the New York season of the Ballet Russe de Monte Carlo, which makes use of railroad work songs and fiddle tunes as well as cowboy songs proper. This western material seemed to bring Copland's mature style to fruition as representative of the many popular idioms of US music. However when he came to compose *Appalachian Spring* for Martha Graham (1942-44), set in a Puritan community of 19th-century Pennsylvania, he added fresh resources to his palette in the form of East Coast hymnody, culminating in the variations on the Shaker song 'Tis a gift to be simple'. All three of these ballets also contain episodes of clear, pellucid, pastoral reverie which seem as characteristic of Copland as any of the more exuberant moments.

Copland continued to compose works on Western themes - the film score *The Red Pony* (1948) is a junior offspring of *Billy the Kid* and *Rodeo* - and was even to write one further 'Western ballet', though that takes the shape of the dances in the graduation party scene in his opera *The Tender Land* (1952-54). His last ballet score as such, *Dance Panels* (1959-62) for Jerome Robbins, is on one level a more abstract score, a sequence of dances without specific story or setting. But while its idiom is more austere than the ballets of the 1930s and 1940s, and though it includes no references to folksong or hymnody, the spirit of jazz still enlivens its rhythms, and the clear, spacious textures hark back to *Billy the Kid*'s evocations of far Western horizons in the clear air.

Malcolm MacDonald

Préface

C'est en grande partie dans ses compositions pour la danse - le ballet et la musique se rapportant aux airs de danses et à leurs formes - qu'Aaron Copland trouva son style particulier et devint l'un des compositeurs américains les plus typiques du XXème siècle. Alors que ses trois principaux ballets « américains » - *Billy the Kid*, *Rodeo* et *Appalachian Spring* - ont été écrits au cours d'une période relativement courte, entre 1938 et 1944, son intérêt pour la danse remonte aux années 20 et persiste jusque dans les années 60.

En 1922-24, alors qu'il étudiait avec Nadia Boulanger à Paris, il écrivit un ballet en un acte – sa première œuvre orchestrale - portant le titre de *Grohg* et basé sur le célèbre film d'horreur allemand *Nosferatu,* de Murnau. Ce ballet ne fut jamais représenté du vivant de Copland, mais il en tira la *Dance Symphony* avec laquelle il gagna son premier prix important, le prix de l'enregistrement de RCA Victor en 1929. Malgré une inspiration germano-expressioniste, la musique du ballet et de la symphonie illustre à quel point le jeune Copland est convaincu du potentiel qu'offrent le jazz et le blues. Il explore ces styles plus avant dans un grand nombre de ses œuvres ultérieures, telles que *Music for the Theater* (1925) avec ses morceaux de 'Danse' et 'Burlesque' et dans son deuxième ballet *Hear Ye! Hear Ye!* (1934). Ce dernier fut son premier ballet sur un sujet américain - un drame satirique dans une salle de tribunal où est jugé un meurtre commis dans un nightclub, le tout dans un style de jazz approprié. *El salón México* (1936), qui lui fut inspiré par la visite d'une salle de bal de Mexico, et qui contient des airs du folklore mexicain, marque l'entrée dans son style personnel de la musique traditionnelle latino-américaine. Plus tard, il composa des œuvres dans un style similaire, *Danzón Cubano* (1942), qui évoque la danse indigène cubaine, et les morceaux de danse mexicains et vénézuéliens qui forment les *Three Latin-American Sketches* (1959-71).

Ainsi, lorsqu'il se mit à composer *Billy the Kid* en 1938 pour la compagnie d'avant-garde « Ballet Caravan » de Lincoln Kirstein, Copland était déjà expert dans l'utilisation de la musique traditionnelle. Il s'était inspiré du « Old West » l'année précédente, pour sa composition pour radio *Prairie Journal*, et il a pu incorporer plusieurs chansons authentiques de cow-boy dans le nouveau ballet (ainsi qu'un peu plus de musique mexicaine). Il continua avec ce procédé dans *Rodeo* (1942), composé pour la saison new-yorkoise de Ballet Russe de Monte Carlo, qui utilise des chants de cheminots et des airs de violon, ainsi que d'authentiques chansons de cow-boy. Cette musique de l'Ouest du pays permet au style de Copland de se développer et de devenir le représentant des nombreux langages musicaux populaires des Etats-Unis. Cependant, quand il composa *Appalachian Spring* pour Martha Graham (1942-44), qui se situe dans une communauté puritaine de la Pennsylvanie du XIXème siècle, il ajouta des touches fraîches à sa palette sous la forme de cantiques de la côte Est, qui culminent dans les variations sur le chant des Shakers « Tis a gift to be simple ». Les trois ballets contiennent aussi des moments de rêverie claire, limpide et pastorale qui semblent aussi caractéristiques de la musique de Copland que ses moments plus exubérants.

Copland continua de composer des œuvres sur les thèmes de l'Ouest américain - la musique du film *The Red Pony* (1948) est de la même famille que *Billy the Kid* et *Rodeo* - et composa un nouveau « ballet de l'Ouest », bien que celui-ci prenne la forme de danses dans la scène de la distribution des prix de son opéra *The Tender Land* (1952-54). Sa dernière composition pour le ballet proprement dit, *Dance Panels* (1959-62) pour Jerome Robbins, est à un certain niveau, une composition plus abstraite, une séquence de danses sans histoire et sans cadre. Mais, alors que son style est plus austère que dans les ballets des années 30 et 40, et qu'il ne fait aucune référence au folkore ou aux cantiques, on retrouve dans son rythme la vivacité de l'esprit du jazz, et les textures vastes et claires rappellent les évocations du Far West de *Billy the Kid*.

Malcolm MacDonald

Vorwort

Aaron Copland verdankt seinen Ruf, einer der bekanntesten Vertreter neuer amerikanischer Musik des 20. Jahrhunderts zu sein, zum größten Teil seinen Tanzwerken - sowohl den Balletten als auch seiner Musik, die sich auf Tanzmelodien und -formen bezieht. In diesen Werken fand Copland zu seinem unverkennbaren Stil. Zwar entstanden seine drei bedeutendsten „amerikanischen" Ballette *Billy the Kid, Rodeo* und *Appalachian Spring* in einem verhältnismäßig kurzen Zeitraum zwischen 1938 und 1944, doch bewahrte Copland von den 20er bis zu den 60er Jahren sein Interesse an der Tanzmusik.

Während seiner kompositorischen Ausbildung in Paris bei Nadia Boulanger komponierte Copland 1922-24 sein erstes Orchesterwerk, das Ballett *Grohg* in einem Akt, für das er Murnaus berühmten Horrorfilm *Nosferatu* als Vorlage benutzte. Das Ballett wurde zwar zu Coplands Lebzeiten nicht aufgeführt, aus ihm stammt aber die *Dance Symphony*, mit der er 1929 seinen ersten großen Preis, einen RCA-Victor-Aufnahmepreis, gewann. Die Musik im Ballett des jungen Copland ist von Jazz- und Blues-Elementen geprägt, trotz des deutsch-expressionistischen Hintergrundes. Mit diesen Stilen experimentierte der Komponist dann auch in vielen späteren Werken, z. B. in *Music for the Theater* (1925) mit seinen tänzerischen und burlesken Elementen und in seinem zweiten Ballett *Hear Ye! Hear Ye!* (1934). Dieses Stück war sein erstes Ballett auf ein amerikanisches Sujet: ein satirisches Theaterstück in einem Gerichtssaal, in dem über einen Mord in einem Nachtclub verhandelt wird; das alles im passenden Jazzstil. Mit *El salón México* (1936), inspiriert durch den Besuch in einem Tanzsaal in Mexiko City und mit authentischen mexikanischen Folkloreelementen durchsetzt, beginnt Coplands Integration lateinamerikanischer Volksmusik in sein ganz persönliches Idiom. Spätere Partituren ähnlichen Stils sind der *Danzón Cubano* (1942), ein Stück, das an einen kubanischen Tanz erinnert, und die mexikanischen und venezuelanischen Tanzstücke, die in den *Three Latin-American Sketches* (1959-71) zusammengefaßt sind.

Als Copland schließlich 1938 für Lincoln Kirsteins Pioniergruppe „Ballet Caravan" *Billy the Kid* komponierte, hatte er schon viel Erfahrung mit folkloristischem Material. Im Jahr zuvor hatte er seinen Blick gen Westen gerichtet, um Material für seine Radiomusik für Orchester *Prairie Journal* zu sammeln, und konnte so mehrere authentische Cowboy-Songs sowie weiteres mexikanisches Material in das neue Ballett einarbeiten. Diese Vorgehensweise wandte er auch bei *Rodeo* (1942) an, das er für die New Yorker Saison des Ballet Russe de Monte Carlo komponierte und in das er Arbeits-Songs von Bahnarbeitern, Fiedelmelodien sowie echte Cowboy-Songs einarbeitete. Dieses Material aus dem Westen schien Coplands reifen Stil zu vollenden und ihn damit zu einem Vertreter der vielen bekannten Idiome amerikanischer Musik zu machen. Als er jedoch in *Appalachian Spring* (1942-44), komponiert für Martha Graham, eine puritanischen Gemeinschaft im Pennsylvania des 19. Jahrhunderts porträtierte, erweiterte er seine musikalischen Mittel durch Ostküsten-Melodien, die schließlich in den Variationen des Shaker-Liedes „Tis a gift to be simple" zum Ausdruck kamen. Alle drei Ballette enthalten auch pastoral-träumerische Episoden, die ebenso typisch für Copland sind wie die ausgelasseneren Momente.

Copland komponierte auch weiterhin Werke mit Wildwest-Thematik. Die Filmmusik *The Red Pony* (1948) ist eng verwandt mit *Billy the Kid* und *Rodeo*. Der Komponist schrieb später sogar noch ein weiteres „Western-Ballett", das allerdings eher den Tänzen in der Abschlußfeierszene seiner Oper *The Tender Land* (1952-54) entspricht. Seine letzte Ballettpartitur im eigentlichen Sinn, *Dance Panels* (1959-62) für Jerome Robbins, ist eine abstraktere Partitur, nämlich eine Folge von Tänzen ohne besonderes Sujet. Während Coplands musikalische Sprache hier nüchterner ist als in den Balletten der 30er und 40er Jahre und ohne Bezüge zu Folklore oder Hymnen, wird der Rhythmus durch den Geist des Jazz belebt. Die klaren, raumgreifenden musikalischen Gestalten wecken Erinnerungen an *Billy the Kid* mit dem weiten Horizont in der klaren Luft des Wilden Westens.

Malcolm MacDonald

BILLY THE KID

NOTE

This Suite is taken from the ballet *Billy the Kid* written for the American Ballet Caravan at the suggestion of its director Lincoln Kirstein and based on a story by Eugene Loring. The following is a quotation from an article by Aaron Copland 'Notes on a Cowboy Ballet'. "The action begins and closes on the open prairie. The central portion of the ballet concerns itself with significant moments in the life of Billy the Kid. The first scene is a street in a frontier town. Familiar figures amble by. Cowboys saunter into town, some on horseback, others with their lassos. Some Mexican women do a jarabe which is interrupted by a fight between two drunks. Attracted by the gathering crowd, Billy is seen for the first time as a boy of twelve with his mother. The brawl turns ugly, guns are drawn, and in some unaccountable way, Billy's mother is killed. Without an instant's hesitation, in cold fury, Billy draws a knife from a cowhand's sheath and stabs his mother's slayers. His short but famous career had begun. In swift succession we see episodes in Billy's later life. At night, under the stars, in a quiet card game with his outlaw friends. Hunted by a posse led by his former friend Pat Garrett. Billy is pursued. A running gun battle ensues. Billy is captured. A drunken celebration takes place. Billy in prison is, of course, followed by one of Billy's legendary escapes. Tired and worn in the desert, Billy rests with his girl. (Pas de deux). Starting from a deep sleep, he senses movement in the shadows. The posse has finally caught up with him. It is the end."

Section Listing

Instrumentation

Piccolo
2 Flutes
2 Oboes
2 Clarinets in B♭
2 Bassoons

4 Horns in F
3 Trumpets in B♭
3 Trombones
Tuba
Timpani

*Percussion (5)
Harp
Piano
Strings

*glockenspiel, xylophone, cymbals, sleigh bells, triangle, guiro, wood block, temple block, whip, bass drum, side drum, tin whistle

Duration: c. 20 minutes

NOTE

Cette Suite est tirée du ballet *Billy the Kid*, écrit pour la compagnie américaine « Ballet Caravan » sur la suggestion de son directeur Lincoln Kirstein, et inspiré par une nouvelle d'Eugene Loring. Ce qui suit est un extrait d'un article d'Aaron Copland intitulé 'Notes on a Cowboy Ballet'. « L'action commence et se termine dans la grande prairie. La partie centrale du ballet concerne des moments importants de la vie de Billy the Kid. La première scène se situe dans une rue d'une ville frontalière. Des personnages familiers se promènent. Des cow-boys arrivent en ville, certains à cheval, d'autres avec leurs lassos. Des femmes mexicaines font un « jarabe », qui est interrompu par une bagarre entre deux ivrognes. Attiré par l'attroupement, Billy que l'on voit pour la première fois, est un garçon de douze ans accompagné par sa mère. La querelle s'envenime, on dégaine les pistolets et par un jeu de circonstances incompréhensible, la mère de Billy est tuée. Sans un instant d'hésitation, dans une colère blanche, Billy tire un couteau du fourreau d'un cow-boy et poignarde les meurtriers de sa mère. Sa courte mais célèbre carrière vient de commencer. Nous voyons défiler une rapide succession d'épisodes de la vie ultérieure de Billy. La nuit sous les étoiles, c'est un jeu de cartes avec ses amis hors-la-loi. Traqué par un détachement d'hommes dirigé par un de ses anciens amis Pat Garrett. Billy est poursuivi. Une poursuite à coups de pistolet s'ensuit. Billy est capturé. Une fête d'ivrognes a lieu. Billy est en prison, suivi bien sûr d'une de ses évasions légendaires. Fatigué et épuisé dans le désert, Billy se repose avec sa fiancée (Pas de deux). Réveillé en sursaut d'un profond sommeil, il devine des mouvements dans l'ombre. Le détachement l'a finalement rattrapé. C'est la fin. »

ANMERKUNG

Diese Suite stammt aus dem Ballett *Billy the Kid*, das für die amerikanische „Ballet Caravan" auf Vorschlag ihres Direktors Lincoln Kirstein komponiert wurde. Als Vorlage für das Ballett diente eine Erzählung von Eugene Loring. Das folgende Zitat stammt aus einem Artikel von Aaron Copland mit dem Titel „Notes on a Cowboy Ballet" (Anmerkungen zu einem Cowboy-Ballett). „Die Handlung beginnt und endet in der offenen Prärie. Der zentrale Teil des Balletts befaßt sich mit bedeutenden Momenten im Leben von Billy the Kid. Die erste Szene spielt auf der Straße in einer Grenzstadt. Typische Bewohner der Stadt schlendern vorbei. Cowboys kommen in die Stadt, einige auf Pferden, andere mit ihren Lassos. Ein paar mexikanische Frauen tanzen einen Jarabe, der durch einen Kampf zwischen zwei Betrunkenen unterbrochen wird. Angezogen von der sich versammelnden Menge, erscheint Billy erstmals als Zwölfjähriger zusammen mit seiner Mutter auf der Bühne. Die Schlägerei verschärft sich, Pistolen werden gezückt und Billys Mutter wird aus nicht ganz nachzuvollziehendem Grund erschossen. Ohne auch nur eine Sekunde zu zögern und völlig von Wut übermannt, zieht Billy ein Messer aus der Messerscheide eines Hilfscowboys und ersticht die Mörder seiner Mutter. Sein kurzes, aber berühmtes Leben nimmt damit seinen Lauf. In schneller Folge sieht man Episoden aus Billys späterem Leben. In der Nacht unter dem Sternenhimmel, beim Kartenspiel mit seinen geächteten Freunden. Gejagt von einer Gruppe von Verfolgern mit seinem früheren Freund Pat Garrett als Anführer. Billy wird verfolgt. Ein Kleinkrieg beginnt. Billy wird gefangengenommen. Eine feuchtfröhliche Feier findet statt. An eine Szene mit Billy im Gefängnis schließt sich natürlich eine seiner legendären Fluchten an. Müde und erschöpft ruht sich Billy in der Wüste mit seinem Mädchen aus (Pas de deux). Billy wird aus dem Tiefschlaf durch eine Bewegung im Schatten geweckt. Die Verfolger haben ihn schließlich eingeholt. Es ist vorbei."

Aaron Copland working by candlelight

Photo: Victor Kraft

BILLY THE KID

BALLET-SUITE

Introduction: The Open Prairie

AARON COPLAND

Picc.
Fl. 1 2
Ob. 1 2
Clar. 1 2
Bsn 1 2
Hr.
Trpt 1 2 3
Trb. 1 2 3
Tb.
Timp.
B. Drum.
Harp.
Piano
Vl. 1 2
Vla.
Vlc.
Cb.
solo
p cantabile
soli
p poco marc.
con sordino
p poco marc.
pp
ppp
pp
1
unis
p poco marc.
unis.
p poco marc.
p poco marcato

Fl. 1 2
Ob. 1 2
Clar. 1 2
Bsn. 1 2
Hr. 1 2 3 4
Trpt. 1 2 3
Trb. 1 2 3
Tb.
Timp.
Harp.
Piano
Vl. 1 2
Vla.
Vlc.
Cb.
solo
pp espressivo
p
mp
solo
(senza sordino)
p espr.
con sordino
p
p poco marc.
2
div.
(unis.)
div.

Picc.
Fl. 1 2
Ob 1 2
Clar. 1 2
Bsn 1 2
Hr.
Trpt. 1 2 3
Trb. 1 2 3
Tb.
Timp.
B.Drum.
Harp.
Piano
Vl. 1 2
Vla.
Vlc.
Cb.
solo
p
mp
solo p espressivo
(1st con sordino)
p poco pesante
con sordino
solo
senza sordino
unis.

Picc.
Fl. 1 2
Ob. 1 2
1°
Clar. 1 2
Bsn. 1 2
a2
Hr.
Trpt. 1 2 3
(senza sordino)
cresc.
Trb. 1 2 3
Tb.
Timp.
B. Dr.
Harp
Piano
3
Vl. 1 2
senza sordino
Vla.
Vlc.
Cb.

Picc.
Fl. 1 2
a2
Ob. 1 2
solo
mp
cresc. poco a poco
Clar. 1 2
a2
Bsn. 1 2
a2
solo
mp
cresc. poco a poco
ff
Hr.
senza sordino
mp subito
cresc.
Trp 1 2 3
mf
mp subito
cresc.
Trb. 1 2 3
Tb.
Timp.
Cymb.
B. Drum
Harp.
mp
4
(div.)
div.
Vl. 1 2
mp subito
mp
Vla.
Vlc.
senza sord.
mp subito
Cb.
arco
fff

Picc.
Fl. 1 2
Ob. 1 2
Clar. 1 2
Bsn. 1 2
Hr.
Trpt. 1 2 3
Trb. 1 2 3
Tb.
Timp.
Harp.
Piano
Vl. 1 2
Vla.
Vlc.
Cb.
a2
ff marcato
unis.
cresc.
8va
5

Street in a Frontier Town
Moderato 𝅗𝅥 = 100
Picc.
Fl. 1 2
Ob. 1 2
Clar. 1 2
Bsn. 1 2
Hr.
Trpt. 1 2 3
Trb. 1 2 3
Tb.
Timp.
Tin Whistle
Cymbals
B. Drum.
Piano
Vl. 1 2
Vla.
Vlc.
C.b.
a2
stacc.
mp nonchalantly
Tin Whistle only in stage performance
6 Moderato 𝅗𝅥 = 100
dim.

Picc.
Fl. 1
Bsn. 1
Tin Whistle
Vl.
Vla.
solo
mp
p
rit.
a tempo
Clar. 1
Bsn.
Trgl.
Harp.
Piano
p solo
stacc.
(Trgl.)
sfp
7
pizz.
(pizz.)
arco
sf
Vlc.
C.b.

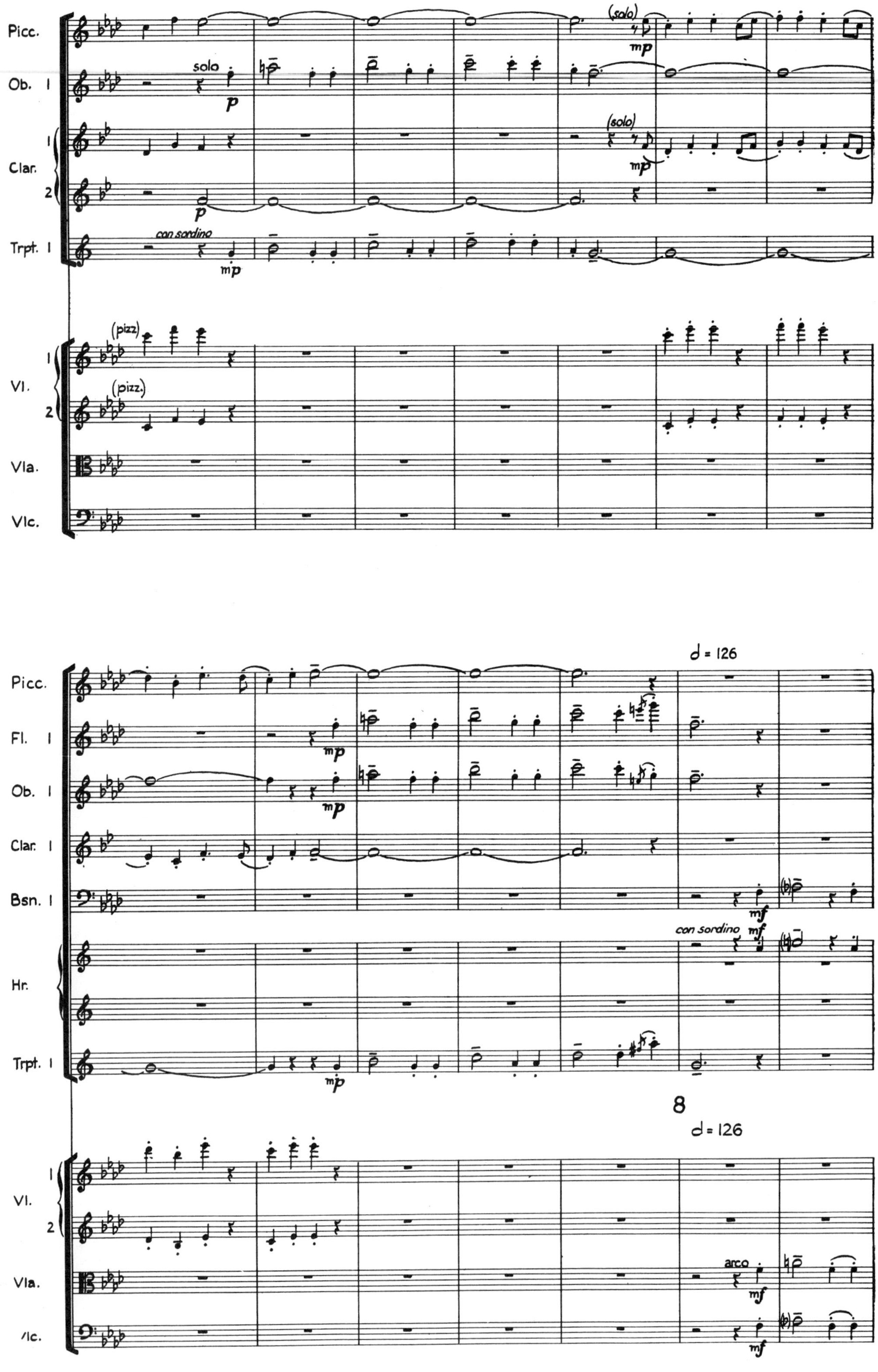

Picc.

Fl. 1

Ob. 1

Clar. 1

Bsn. 1

Hr.

Trpt. 1

Vl. 1 2

Vla.

Vlc.

mp

mf

con sordino

arco

8

𝅗𝅥 = 126

Picc.
Fl. 2
Ob. 2
Clar. 2
Bsn. 2
Hr.
Piano
Vl. 1
2
Vla.
Vlc.

a2
stacc.
p solo
1st solo
soli
p
p stacc.

9

Picc.
Fl.
Ob.
Clar.
Bsn.
Hr.
Trpt.
Trb.
Tb.
Timp.
Piano
Vl.
Vla.
Vlc.
Cb.
(a2)
a2
(senza sord.)
con sordino

Picc.
Fl.
Ob.
Clar.
Bsn.
Hr.
Trpt.
Trb.
Tb.
Timp.
Piano
Vl.
Vla.
Vlc.
Cb.
a2
senza sord.
stacc.
pizz
10

Bsn. 1 2
Hr.
Trb. I
solo
mf poco marcato
Piano
mf stacc.
Vl. 1 2
Vla.
Vlc.
Cb.
Bsn. 1 2
Hr.
Trb. I
Piano
Vl. 1 2
mp
mp
Vla.
mp
Vlc.
mp
Cb.
mp

Picc.
Fl. 1 2
Ob. 1 2
Clar. 1 2
Bsn. 1 2
Hr.
(senza sord.) solo
mf
Trpt. 1 2 3
con sordino
p
Trb. 1 2 3
con sordino
p
con sordino
p
Tb.
con sordino
p
Timp.
stacc.
mf
Piano
11
Vl. 1 2
Vla.
Vlc.
Cb.

Picc.
Fl. 1 2
1° solo
Ob. 1 2
Clar. 1 2
1° solo
Bsn. 1 2
Hr.
Trpt. 1 2 3
Trb. 1 2 3
Tb.
Timp.
Perc.
Piano
Vl. 1 2
div.
pizz.
Vla.
pizz.
Vlc.
arco
Cb.
arco

Picc.
Fl. 1 2
Ob. 1 2
Clar. 1 2
Bsn. 1 2
Hr.
Trpt. 1 2 3
Trb. 1 2 3
Tb.
Timp.
Perc.
Piano
Vl. 1 2
Vla.
Vlc.
Cb.
(1o)
solo
mp
f
12
unis. IV
arco IV

Picc.
Fl. 1 2
Ob. 1 2
Clar. 1 2
Bsn. 1 2
Hr.
Trpt. 1 2 3
Trb. 1 2 3
Tb.
Timp.
Perc.
Piano
Vl. 1 2
Vla.
Vlc.
Cb.
solo
pizz.
mp
mf
f

Fl. 1 2
Clar. 1 2
Bsn 1 2
Hr.
Trpt. 1
Trb. 1
Piano
meno f
solo
con sordino
(senza sord.)
13
Vl.
Vla.
Vlc.
Cb.
(pizz.)
p dim. sempre
pp
ppp

Picc.
Fl. 1 2
Ob. 1 2
Clar. 1 2
Bsn. 1 2
Hr.
Trpt. 1 2 3
Trb. 1 2 3
Tb.
Timp.
Cymb.
B.Drum.
Piano
14
Vl. 1 2
Vla.
Vlc.
Cb.
ff marcato
a2
senza sordino
with hard stick
arco
div.

Picc.
Fl. 1 2
a2
Ob. 1 2
a2
Clar. 1 2
Bsn. 1 2
Hr.
Trpt. 1 2 3
Trb. 1 2 3
Tb.
Timp.
Cymb.
B. Drum
Piano
Vl. 1 2
Vla.
Vlc.
Cb.
ff
sf

♩= 𝅗𝅥 precedente. (♩= 138)
Picc.
Fl. 1 2
Ob. 1 2
a2
Clar. 1 2
Bsn. 1 2
f stacc.
Hr.
f stacc.
f stacc.
Trpt. 1 2 3
Trb. 1 2 3
f stacc.
senza sordino
f stacc.
Tb.
senza sordino
f stacc.
Timp.
Wood-bl.
f
mf
Sn. Drum
f
Cymb.
B. Drum.
Piano
♩= 𝅗𝅥 precedente. (♩= 138)
15
Vl 1 2
f
div.
f
Vla.
f
Vlc.
pizz.
f
Cb.
pizz.
f

Picc.
Fl. 1 2
Ob. 1 2
Clar. 1 2
Bsn. 1 2
a2 stacc.
f
Hr.
Trpt. 1
2 3
solo f
solo f
Trb. 1 2
3
Tb.
Timp.
Woodbl.
Cymb.
B.Drum.
Piano
Vl. 1
2
Vla.
Vlc.
arco
f
Cb.

Picc.
Fl. 1 2
Ob. 1 2
Clar. 1 2
Bsn. 1 2
a2
mf
Hr.
Trpt. 1 2 3
stacc.
Trb. 1 2 3
soli
3
mf legato, cantabile
Tb.
Timp.
Woodbl.
Cymb.
B.Drum.
Piano
16
Vla. 1 2
unis.
pizz.
Vla
Vlc.
arco
Cb.
(pizz)

Picc.
Fl. 1 2
Ob. 1 2
Clar. 1 2
Bsn 1 2
a2
Hr.
Trpt. 1
2 3
Trb. 1 2
3
mf
Tb.
Timp.
Woodbl.
Piano
Vl. 1
2
Vla.
Vlc.
Cb.

Picc.
Fl. 1 2
a2
f
Ob. 1 2
Clar. 1 2
a2
f
Bsn. 1 2
a2
Hr.
f
f
Trpt. 1
2 3
Trb. 1 2
3
3
3
f
Tb.
f
Timp.
Woodbl.
f
Piano
arco
Vl. 1
2
f
div.
arco
f
arco
Vla.
f
(arco)
Vlc.
f
(arco)
C.b.
f

Picc.
Fl. 1 2
a2
Ob. 1 2
Clar. 1 2
Bsn. 1 2
Hr.
con sordino
mf
Trpt. 1
con sordino
solo
Trpt. 2 3
Trb. 1 2
Trb. 3
Tb.
Timp.
Woodbl.
Piano
17
Vl. 1
Vl. 2
Vla.
Vlc.
Cb.

Ob. 1 2
Clar. 1 2
Hr. 1
Trpt. 1
Perc.
Piano
Vl. 1 2
Vla.
a2
mf
Picc.
Fl. 1 2
solo
mf stacc.
1° solo
Sleigh-bells
p
18
Vlc.
pizz.

Picc.
Fl. 1 2
Ob. 1 2
Clar. 1 2
Bsn. 1 2
Hr.
Trpt. 1 2 3
Trb. 1 2 3
Tb.
Timp.
Sleigh-b.
Woodbl.
Piano
Vl. 1 2
Vla.
V'lc.
Cb.
mf
a2

Picc.
Fl. 1 2
a2
f
Ob. 1 2
f
Clar. 1 2
f
Bsn. 1 2
f
Hr.
solo
f cantabile
solo
f cantabile
Trpt.
mf
Trb.
solo
f cantabile
mf
mf
Tb.
mf
Timp.
Perc.
Piano
19
Vl.
f
f
Vla.
f legato, cantabile
tenuto
Vlc.
arco
f legato, cantabile
tenuto
Cb.
arco
div.
mf

Picc.
Fl. 1 2
Ob. 1 2
Clar. 1 2
Bsn. 1 2
Hr.
Trpt.
Trb.
Tb.
Timp.
Perc.
Vl.
Vla.
Vlc.
Cb.

Mexican Dance and Finale

Picc.
Fl. 1 2
Ob. 1 2
Clar. 1 2
Bsn. 1 2
10
Hr.
Trpt. 1 2 3
Trb. 1 2 3
Tb.
Timp.
Woodbl.
Gourd.
Piano
Vl. 1 2
Vla.
Vlc.
Cb.

Picc.
Fl. 1 2
Ob. 1 2
Clar. 1 2
Bsn. 1 2
Hr.
1
Trpt.
2 3
1 2
Trb.
3
Tb.
Timp.
Woodbl.
gourd.
Piano
21
1
Vl.
2
Vla.
Vlc.
Cb.

Picc.
Fl. 1 2
Ob. 1 2
Clar. 1 2
Bsn. 1 2
Hr.
Trpt. 1 2 3
Trb. 1 2 3
Tb.
Timp.
Woodbl.
Gourd.
Piano
Vl. 1 2
Vla.
Vlc.
Cb.

Picc.
Fl.
Ob.
Clar.
Bsn.
Hr.
Trpt.
Trb.
Tb.
Timp.
Woodbl.
Gourd.
Piano
Vl.
Vla.
Vlc.
Cb.
solo
22
modo ordinario
pizz.

Picc.
Fl.
1
2
Ob. 1 2
Clar. 1 2
Bsn. 1 2
1°
Hr.
Trpt.
1
2 3
Trb.
1 2
3
Tb.
Timp.
Woodbl.
Gourd.
Piano
23
Vl.
1
2
Vla
Vlc.
Cb.

Picc.
Fl. 1/2
Ob. 1/2
Clar. 1/2
Bsn. 1/2
1°
Hr.
Trpt. 1
2/3
Trb. 1/2
3
Tb.
Timp.
Woodbl.
Gourd.
Piano
Vl. 1
2
Vla
Vlc.
Cb.
col legno
col legno
col legno
(pizz)

Picc.
Fl. 1 2
Ob. 1 2
Clar. 1 2
Bsn. 1 2
10
Hr.
1
Trpt.
2 3
1 2
Trb.
3
Tb.
Timp.
Woodbl.
Gourd.
Piano
1
Vl.
2
Vla.
Vlc
Cb.

Fl. 1 2
mp
Ob. 1 2
Clar. 1 2
mp
Hr.
mf
mp
mf
mp
Trpt. 1
2 3

24

Vl. 1
arco
legato
mf
Vl. 2
modo ordinario
mf
Vla.
modo ordinario
mf
Vlc.
arco
modo ordinario
mf

Ob. 1 2
Clar. 1 2
Bsn. 1 2
Hr.
25
Vl. 1 2
Vla.
Vlc.
solo mp
p
(dim.)
sul G....
mp

Ob. 1 2
Clar. 1 2
Bsn. 1 2
Hr.
Vl. 1 2
Vla.
Vlc.
mf
p
(sul G)
pizz.
p

Fl. 1 2
Ob. 1 2
Clar. 1 2
Bsn. 1 2
Glocksp.
mf
a2
(sounds 8va higher)
p
25A
Vl.
1
2
Vla.
Vlc.
arco
mf
mp
Hr.
senza sordino
(con sordino)
p

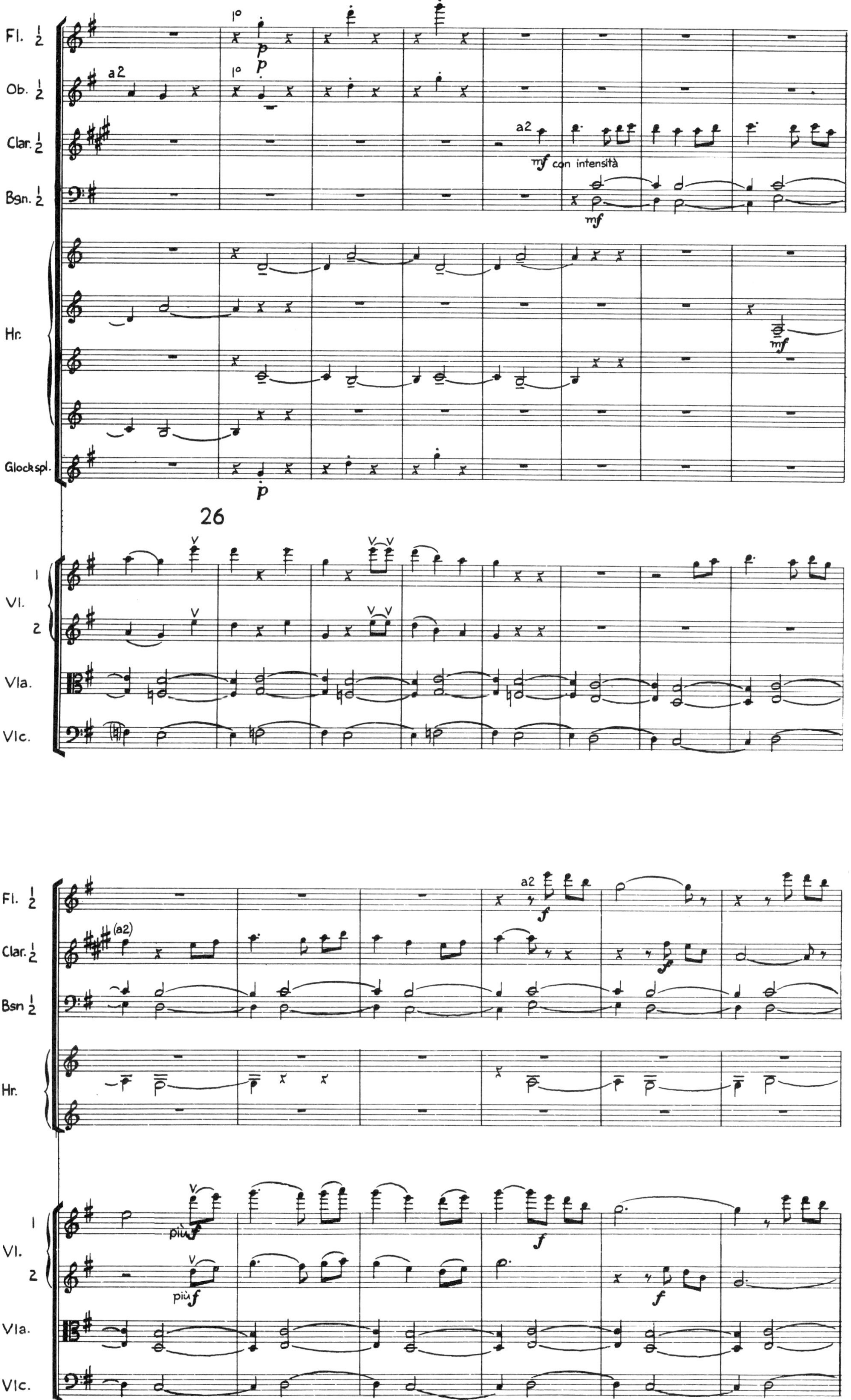

Fl. 1/2
1° *p*
Ob. 1/2
a2 1° *p*
Clar. 1/2
a2 *mf* con intensità
Bgn. 1/2
mf
Hr.
mf
Glockspl.
p
26
Vl. 1 2
Vla.
Vlc.

Picc
Fl. 1 2
(a2)
Ob. 1 2
a2
Clar. 1 2
(a2)
Bsn. 1 2
Hr.
senza sordino
Trpt. 1 2 3
solo
Trb. 1 2 3
Tb.
Timp.
Perc.
Piano
26A
Vl. 1 2
Vla.
Vlc.
Cb.
(arco)

Picc.
Fl. 1 2
Ob. 1 2
Clar. 1 2
Bsn. 1 2
Hr.
Trpt. 1 2 3
Trb. 1 2 3
Tb.
Timp.
Perc.
Piano
Vl. 1 2
Vla.
Vlc.
Cb.
(a2)
a2
stacc.
marc.
senza sordino
senza sord.
ff

Picc.
Fl. 1 2
(a2)
Ob. 1 2
Clar. 1 2
Bsn. 1 2
Hr.
Trpt. 1 2 3
Trb. 1 2 3
Tb.
Timp.
Glockspl.
Xyloph.
Cymb. B. Drum.
Piano
8va
27
Vl. 1 2
Vla.
Vlc.
Cb.

Picc.
Fl. 1 2
(a2)
Ob. 1 2
Clar. 1 2
Bsn. 1 2
Hr.
Trpt. 1 2 3
fff
Trb. 1 2 3
Tb.
Timp.
Glockspl.
Xyloph.
Cymb. B.Drum
ff
Piano
8va
Vl. 1 2
Vla.
Vlc.
Cb.

meno mosso
Picc.
Fl. 1 2
Ob. 1 2
Clar. 1 2
Bsn 1 2
Hr.
Trpt. 1 2 3
Trb. 1 2 3
Tb.
Timp.
Glockspl.
Xyloph.
Slapstick
Cymb. B.Drum.
Piano
27A
meno mosso
Vl. 1 2
Vla.
Vlc.
Cb.
(a2)
a2
div.
pizz.
arco

Slowly
Ob. I
Bsn. I
solo
p espr.
pp espr.
p espr.
28 Slowly
Vlc.
Cb.
pp
ppp
Prairie Night (Card game at night)
Molto Moderato (♩. = ♩ prec.)
Fl. I
Ob. I
Bsn. I
p
pp
Molto Moderato (♩. = ♩ prec.)
29
con sord
p dolce, semplice, cantabile
Vl.
Vla.
Vlc.
con sordino
con sordino
espr.
p molto legato
Fl. I
Clar. I
Bsn. I
Cb.

Picc.
Fl. I
Ob. I
Clar. I
Bsn. I
Vl.
Vla.
Vlc.
Picc.
Fl. I
Ob. I
Clar. I
Bsn. I
Trpt. I
Harp.
Vl.
Vla.
Vlc.

Fl. 1
Ob. 1
Clar. 1
Bsn. 1
Trpt. 1
Harp.
solo
(con sord.)
pp
p
solo
30
Vl.
1
2
Vla.
Vlc.
Fl. 1
Ob. 1
Clar. 1
Bsn. 1
Trpt. 1
Harp
Vl.
1
2
Vla.
Vlc.

Fl. I
Bsn. I
Trpt. I
pp marcato poco
pp
solo espressivo
senza sord.
p freely
freely
31
a trifle hurried.
rit.
Vl.
pp
ppp
Vla.
pp
Vlc.
pp
pp

Fl. I
Bsn. I
Trpt. I
short
a trifle hurried.
rit.
Vl.
pp sempre
ppp sempre
Vlc.
pp sempre

Bsn. I
Trpt. I
32
a trifle hurried.
rit.
Vl.
Vlc.

Gun Battle

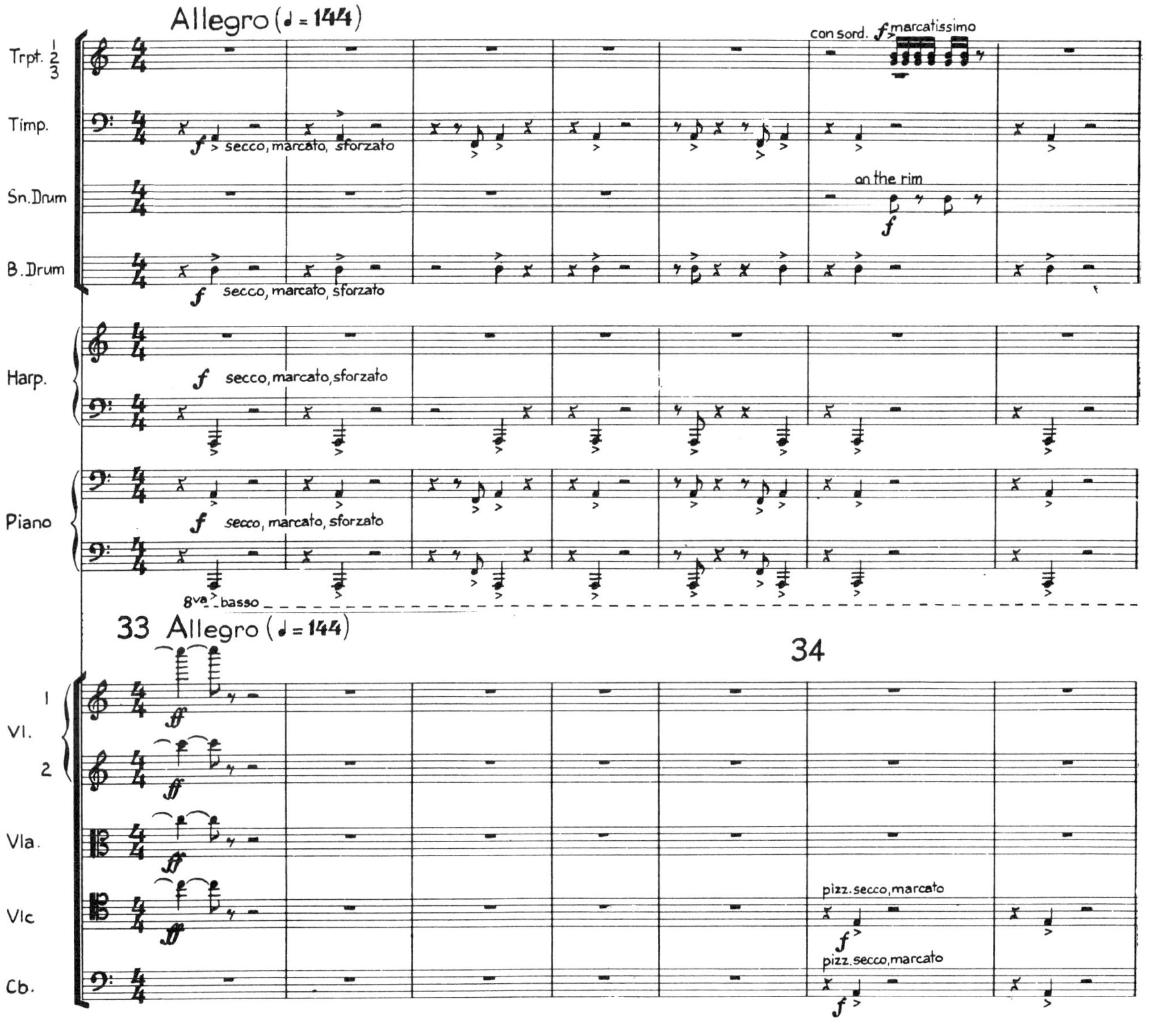

Allegro (♩ = 144)

Trpt. 1 2 3 — con sord. *f* marcatissimo

Timp. — *f* secco, marcato, sforzato

Sn. Drum — on the rim, *f*

B. Drum — *f* secco, marcato, sforzato

Harp. — *f* secco, marcato, sforzato

Piano — *f* secco, marcato, sforzato — 8va basso

33 Allegro (♩ = 144) — 34

Vl. 1, 2 — *ff*

Vla. — *ff*

Vlc — *ff* — pizz. secco, marcato *f*

Cb. — pizz. secco, marcato *f*

Fl. 1
Ob. 1
Clar. 1
Bsn. 1
Hr.
1
Trpt.
2
3
1
2
Trb.
3
Tb.
Timp.
Sn. Drum.
B. Drum.
Harp.
Piano
8va basso
1
Vl.
2
Vla.
Vlc.
Cb.

Picc.
Fl. 1 2
Ob. 1 2
Clar. 1 2
Bsn. 1 2
Hr.
1 Trpt. 2 3
1 2 Trb. 3
Tb.
Timp.
Sn. Drum
B. Drum.
Harp.
Piano
Vl. 1 2
Vla.
Vlc.
Cb.
ff
a2
con sordino
8va
8vabasso
35
divisi
arco

Picc.
Fl. 1/2
Ob. 1/2
Clar. 1/2
Bsn. 1/2
Hr.
Trpt. 1
Trpt. 2/3
Trb. 1/2
Trb. 3
Tb.
Timp.
Sn. Drum
B. Drum
Harp
Piano
Vl. 1
Vl. 2
Vla.
Vlc.
Cb.
marcato, non legato
a2
3rd senza sordino
(2nd con sord.)
(senza sordino)
8va
8va basso
divisi

Picc.
marcato, non legato
Fl. 1 2
(a2)
marcato, non legato
Ob. 1 2
a2
marcato, non legato
Clar. 1 2
a2
marcato, non legato
Bsn. 1 2
Hr.
senza sordino
Trpt. 1 2 3
senza sordino
marcato, non legato
Trb. 1 2 3
Tb.
Timp.
Xyloph.
ff
S. Drum.
B. Drum.
Harp.
Piano
8va
fff non legato
8va basso
Vl. 1 2
Vla.
Vlc.
Cb

Picc.
Fl. 1/2
Ob. 1/2
Clar. 1/2
Bsn. 1/2
Hr.
Trpt. 1 2 3
Trb. 1/2 3
Tb.
Timp.
Xyloph.
Sn. Drum
B. Drum
Harp.
Piano
36
Vl. 1 2
Vla.
Vlc.
Cb
ff
a2
unis.
8va
8va basso

Picc.
Fl. 1 2
Ob. 1 2
Clar. 1 2
Bsn 1 2
Hr.
Trpt. 1 2 3
Trb. 1 2 3
Tb.
Timp.
Xyloph.
Sn. Drum
B. Drum.
Harp.
Piano
Vl. 1 2
Vla.
Vlc.
Cb.
a2
8va
8va basso

Picc.
Fl. 1/2
Ob. 1/2
Clar. 1/2
Bsn. 1/2
Hr.
Trpt. 1 2/3
Trb. 1/2 3
Tb.
Timp.
Xyloph.
Sn. Drum.
B. Drum.
Harp.
Piano
Vl. 1 2
Vla.
Vlc.
Cb.
a2
f
ff
8va
8va basso
37

Picc.
Fl. 1 2
a2
Ob. 1 2
Clar. 1 2
Bsn. 1 2
Hr.
Trpt. 1 2 3
Trb. 1 2 3
Tb.
Timp.
Xyloph.
Sn.Drum
B.Drum
Harp.
Piano
8va
8va basso
Vl. 1 2
Vla.
Vlc.
Cb.
f
ff

Picc.
Fl. 1/2
a2
Flute 2 change to Piccolo 2
Ob. 1/2
a2
Clar. 1/2
a2
Bsn. 1/2
a2
Hr.
Trpt. 1
2 3
3rd
Trb. 1 2
3
Tb.
Timp.
Xyloph.
Sn. Drum
B. Drum.
Harp.
Piano
8va
8va basso
Vl. 1
2
Vla.
Vlc.
Cb.

a2
Bsn 1 2
Hr.
Trpt. 1 2 3
Trb. 1 2 3
Tb.
Timp.
Sn. Drum
B. Drum
Harp.
Piano
8va
8va basso
38
Vl. 1 2
Vla.
Vlc
Cb.
fff

a2
Bsn. 1 2
sf
Trb. 3
sf
Tb.
sf
Timp.
sf
meno f
mf
p
B. Drum.
sf
meno f
mf
p
Harp.
sf
meno f
mf
p
Piano
sf
meno f
mf
p
8va
39
Vlc.
sf.
meno f
Cb.
sf.
meno f
Celebration (after Billy's capture)
Allegro (𝅗𝅥 = 90)
solo
mp
Picc 1 2
Fl. 1
solo
mp
Ob. 1 2
Clar. 1 2
mp
p
Bsn. 1 2
40
Allegro (𝅗𝅥 = 90)
Vl. 1 2
3
mp
Vla
Vlc.
pizz.
Cb.
p

Picc. 1 2
Ob. 1 2
Clar.
Bsn.
Vl.
Vla.
Vlc.
Cb.
mf
a2
mp
Tb.
p
41

Picc. 1 2
a2
Fl. I
Ob. 1 2
a2
Clar. 1 2
Bsn. 1 2
Hr.
Trpt. 1 2 3
con sordino
con sordino
Trb. 1 2 3
Tb.
Timp.
Perc.
Piano
Vl. 1 2
Vla.
Vlc.
Cb.

Picc. 1 2
Fl. 1
Ob. 1 2
Clar. 1 2
Bsn. 1 2
Hr.
Trpt. 1 2 3
Trb. 1 2 3
Tb.
Timp.
Perc.
Piano
Vl. 1 2
Vla.
Vlc.
Cb.
a2
f
mf

Picc. 1 2
Fl. 1
Ob. 1 2
Clar. 1 2
Bsn. 1 2
Hr.
Trpt. 1 2 3
Trb. 1 2 3
Tb.
Timp.
Perc.
Harp.
Piano
Vl. 1 2
Vla
Vlc.
Cb.
a2
con sordino
mf
p
mp
brittle, stacc.
brittle
42
pizz

Picc. 1 2
Fl. 1
solo
stacc.
mf
Ob. 1 2
soli a2
stacc.
mf
Clar. 1 2
solo
stacc.
mf
Bsn. 1 2
Hr.
Trpt. 1
con sordino
f stacc.
Trb. 1 2
3
Tb.
Timp.
Perc
Harp.
Piano
Vl. 1
2
Vla.
Vlc.
Cb.

a2
stacc.
Picc 1 2
Fl. 1
Ob. 1 2
stacc.
Clar. 1 2
Bsn. 1 2
Hr.
1
Trpt.
2 3
1 2
Trb.
3
Tb.
Timp.
stacc.
Xyloph.
B. Drum
Harp.
Piano
43
1
Vl.
2
div.
arco
Vla.
arco
Vlc.
arco
Cb.

Picc. 1 2
a2
Fl. 1
Ob. 1 2
f
Clar. 1 2
Bsn 1 2
Hr.
Trpt. 1 2 3
senza sordino
senza sordino
Trb. 1 2 3
Tb.
Timp.
Xyloph.
B. Drum.
Piano
Vl. 1 2
Vla.
Vlc.
Cb.

Picc. 1 2
Fl. 1
Ob. 1 2
a2
f
Clar. 1 2
Bsn. 1 2
Hr.
Trpt. 1 2 3
Trb. 1 2 3
Tb.
Timp.
Xyloph.
stacc.
B. Drum.
Piano
Vl. 1 2
Vla.
Vlc.
Cb.

Picc. 1 2
Fl. 1
Ob. 1 2
Clar. 1 2
Bsn. 1 2
Hr.
Trpt. 1 2 3
Trb. 1 2 3
Tb.
Timp.
Xyloph.
B.Drum
Piano
Vl. 1 2
Vla.
Vlc.
Cb.
solo p sub.
a2
unis.
44
pizz.
p

Picc. 1 2
Fl. 1
stacc.
p
Ob. 1 2
stacc.
p
Clar. 1 2
Bsn. 1 2
Hr.
Trpt. 1 2 3
Trb. 1 2 3
Tb.
Timp.
Perc.
Piano
Vl. 1 2
p
Vla.
Vlc.
Cb.

Picc. 1 2
Fl. 1
Ob. 1 2
Clar. 1 2
Bsn. 1 2
Hr.
Trpt. 1 2 3
Trb. 1 2 3
Tb.
Timp.
Perc.
Piano
Vl. 1 2
Vla.
Vlc.
Cb.
crudely
1o
mf
con sordino
stacc.
pizz.
45

Picc. 1 2
Fl. 1
Ob. 1 2
Clar. 1 2
Bsn. 1 2
Hr.
con sordino
Trpt. 1 2 3
Trb. 1 2 3
Tb.
Timp.
Xyloph.
secco
Piano.
Vl. 1 2
Vla.
Vlc.
Cb.

Picc.
Fl.
Ob.
Clar.
Bsn.
Hr.
f senza sordino
Trpt.
Trb.
Tb.
Xyloph.
ff
8va
Piano
Vl.
Vla.
Vlc.
Cb.

Picc.
Fl.
Ob.
Clar.
Bsn.
Hr.
senza sordino
Trpt.
Trb.
Tb.
Xyloph.
Piano
8va
Vl.
Vla
Vlc.
Cb.

Picc. 1 2
Fl. 1
Ob. 1 2
Clar. 1 2
Bsn. 1 2
Hr.
Trpt. 1 2 3
Trb. 1 2 3
Tb.
Timp.
Perc.
Harp.
Piano
46
Vl. 1 2
Vla.
Vlc.
Cb.
a2
f
1o
pp
con sordino pp
senza sordino
8va
pp subito
pp

Picc. 1 2
Fl. 1
Ob. 1 2
Clar. 1 2
Bsn. 1 2
Hr.
Trpt. 1 2 3
Trb. 1 2 3
Tb.
Timp.
Cymb.
B.Drum
Piano
Vl. 1 2
Vla.
Vlc.
Cb.
a2
senza sord.
arco

a2
Picc. 1 2
Fl. 1
Ob. 1 2
Clar. 1 2
Bsn. 1 2
Hr.
Trpt. 1 2 3
Trb. 1 2 3
Tb.
Timp.
Sn. Drum
B. Drum.
Piano
47
Vl. 1 2
Vla.
Vlc.
Cb.
più f
f
ff

Picc. 1 2
a2
Fl. 1
Ob. 1 2
a2
Clar. 1 2
Bsn. 1 2
Hr.
1
Trpt. 2
3
1 2
Trb.
3
Tb.
Timp.
Sn. Drum
B. Drum
Piano
1
Vl.
2
Vla
Vlc.
Cb.

Picc. 1 2
a2
Fl. 1
Ob. 1 2
a2
Clar. 1 2
a2♮
Bsn. 1 2
Hr.
Trpt. 1 2 3
Trb. 1 2 3
Tb.
Timp.
Sn. Drum.
B. Drum.
Piano
Vl. 1 2
Vla
Vlc.
Cb.
fff

Picc. 1 2
Fl. 1
Ob. 1 2
Clar. 1 2
Bsn. 1 2
Hr.
Trpt. 1 2 3
Trb. 1 2 3
Tb.
Timp.
Sn. Drum
Cymb. B. Drum.
Piano
48
Vl. 1 2
Vla.
Vlc.
Bb.
a2
fff

Picc. 1 2
a2
Fl. 1
Ob. 1 2
a2
Clar. 1 2
a2
Bsn. 1 2
Hr.
Trpt. 1 2 3
Trb. 1 2 3
Tb.
Timp.
Sn. Drum.
Slapstick.
Cymbals
B. Drum.
Piano
8va
Vl. 1 2
Vla.
Vlc.
Cb.

Billy's Death

Lento Moderato (♩ = 60)

Picc. 1 2

Piccolo 2 change to Flute 2

Fl. 1

Ob. 1 2

Clar. 1 2

Bsn. 1 2

Trpt. 1 2

49 Lento Moderato (♩ = 60)

Solo Violin

solo quasi tremolando

pp

Vl. 1

senza sordino

mf molto espressivo

pp

p

Vl. 2

senza sordino

mf molto espressivo

pp

p

Vla.

senza sordino

mf molto espressivo

pp

p

Vlc.

senza sordino

mf molto espressivo

pp

p

Cb.

senza sordino

mf molto espressivo

pp

p

Picc.
Fl. 1 2
mp
p
Ob. 1 2
Clar. 1 2
1° solo espressivo
mf
p
Bsn. 1 2
Hr.
Trpt. 1
2 3
Trb. 1 2
3
Tb.
Timp.
Perc.
Harp.
p
pp
Piano
50
Solo Violin
pp
Vl. 1
2
mf
p
Vla.
Vlc.
Cb.

♩=54
Picc.
Fl. 1 2
Ob. 1 2
Clar. 1 2
Bsn. 1 2
Hr.
Trpt. 1 2 3
Trb. 1 2 3
Tb.
Timp.
Perc.
Harp
Piano
51
♩=54
Vl. 1 2
Vla
Vlc.
Cb.

Picc.
Fl. 1 2
Ob. 1 2
Clar. 1 2
Bsn. 1 2
Hr
Trpt. 1 2 3
Trb. 1 2 3
Tb.
Timp.
Perc.
Harp.
Piano
Vl. 1 2
Vla
Vlc.
Cb.
mf

Picc.
Fl. 1 2
Ob. 1 2
Clar. 1 2
Bsn. 1 2
Hr.
Trpt. 1 2 3
Trb. 1 2 3
Tb.
Timp.
Perc.
Harp.
Piano
Vl. 1 2
Vla.
Vlc.
Cb.
52
a2
mf
mp
cresc. p. a p.
cresc. poco a poco

Picc.
Fl. 1 2
Ob. 1 2
Clar. 1 2
Bsn. 1 2
Hr.
Trpt. 1 2 3
Trb. 1 2 3
Tb.
Timp.
Perc.
Harp.
Piano
Vl. 1 2
Vla.
Vlc.
Cb.
a2
f
ff
marcato
8va
53

Picc.
Fl. 1 2
Ob. 1 2
Clar. 1 2
Bsn. 1 2
Hr.
Trpt. 1 2
3
Trb. 1 2
3
Tb.
Timp.
Perc.
Harp.
8va
Piano
Vl. 1
2
Vla.
Vlc.
Cb.

Picc.
Fl. 1 2
Ob. 1 2
a2
Clar. 1 2
Bsn. 1 2
Hr.
Trpt. 1 2 3
Trb. 1 2 3
a2
Tb.
Timp.
Cymb.
B.Drum
Harp.
Piano
8va
54
div.
Vl. 1 2
Vla.
Vlc.
Cb.

Picc.
Fl. 1 2
Ob. 1 2
a2
Clar. 1 2
Bsn. 1 2
Hr.
Trpt. 1 2 3
Trb. 1 2 3
a2
Tb.
Timp.
Cymb.
B.Drum.
Harp.
8va
Piano
Vl. 1 2
Vla.
Vlc
Cb.
sff

FOUR DANCE EPISODES *FROM* RODEO

Instrumentation

3 Flutes (2nd & 3rd doubling Piccolo)
2 Oboes
Cor Anglais
2 Clarinets in B♭
Bass Clarinet in B♭
2 Bassoons
4 Horns in F
3 Trumpets in B♭
3 Trombones

Tuba
Timpani
Percussion
xylophone, glockenspiel, cymbal, bass drum, snare drum, wood block, slap stick, triangle
Celeste
Harp
Piano
Strings

Movement Listing

Duration: c. 18 minutes

NOTE

The Ballet Russe de Monte Carlo commissioned the choreographer Agnes de Mille and the composer Aaron Copland to collaborate on the creation of a western ballet for its 1942-43 season. Originally sub-titled *The Courting at Burnt Ranch*, *Rodeo* was first produced at the Metropolitan Opera House on 16 October, 1942, with scenery by Oliver Smith and costumes by Kermit Love.

The idea for the ballet was devised by Agnes de Mille who described it as follows: "Throughout the American Southwest, the Saturday afternoon rodeo is a tradition. On the remote ranches, as well as in the trading centres and the towns, the 'hands' get together to show off their skill in roping, riding, branding and throwing. Often, on the more isolated ranches, the rodeo is done for an audience that consists only of a handful of fellow-workers, women-folk, and those nearest neighbours who can make the eighty or so mile run-over. The afternoon's exhibition is usually followed by a Saturday night dance at the Ranch House. The theme of the ballet is basic. It deals with the problem that has confronted all American women, from earliest pioneer times, and which has never ceased to occupy them throughout the history of the building of our country: how to get a suitable man."

The music was written in June, and orchestrated in September, 1942. The composer subsequently extracted an orchestral suite from the ballet score for concert performance under the title *Four Dance Episodes* from *Rodeo*: I. *Buckaroo Holiday*, II. *Corral Nocturne*, III. *Saturday Night Waltz*, IV. *Hoe-Down*. A number of American folk songs are woven into the score. Source material was drawn from "Our Singing Country" by John A. and Alan Lomax and Ira Ford's "Traditional Music of America". Two songs from the Lomax volume are incorporated into the first Episode: "If he'd be a buckaroo by his trade" and "Sis Joe". The rhythmic oddities of "Sis Joe" provided rich material for reworking. A square dance tune called "Bonyparte" provides the principal theme of the *Hoe-Down*. On the other hand no folk material was drawn upon for the *Corral Nocturne*.

Three Episodes were first performed in a concert by the Boston Pops Orchestra under Arthur Fiedier on 28 May, 1943. The entire suite was premiered by Alexander Smatiens at the Stadium Concerts with the New York Philharmonic Symphony in July, 1943.

NOTE

Le Ballet Russe de Monte Carlo avait fait une commande à la chorégraphe Agnes de Mille et au compositeur Copland pour collaborer à la création d'un ballet-western pour sa saison de 1942-43. Portant à l'origine le sous-titre de *The Courting at Burnt Ranch*, *Rodeo* a été produit tout d'abord par le Metropolitan Opera House le 16 octobre 1942, avec des décors d'Oliver Smith et des costumes de Kermit Love.

L'idée du ballet a été imaginée par Agnes de Mille qui la décrit comme suit : « Partout dans le sud-ouest américain, le rodéo du samedi après-midi est une tradition. Dans les ranchs isolés, ainsi que dans les centres marchands et les villes, les travailleurs sont prêts à montrer leur compétence avec les cordes, à cheval, au marquage des bêtes, au lancer. Souvent dans les ranchs isolés, des rodéos sont organisés pour un public qui consiste seulement en une poignée de compagnons de travail, de femmes du pays et de voisins qui peuvent faire les cent vingt kilomètres de parcours. L'après-midi d'épreuves est suivi habituellement par un bal organisé dans la maison du ranch. Le thème du ballet est simple. Il traite du problème auquel sont confrontées toutes les femmes américaines depuis le temps des premiers pionniers, et qui n'a jamais cessé de les préoccuper dans toute l'histoire de la construction de notre pays : comment se procurer un homme convenable. »

La musique fut écrite en juin et orchestrée en septembre 1942. Le compositeur tira plus tard une suite orchestrale du ballet sous le nom de *Four Dance Episodes from Rodeo* : I. *Buckaroo Holiday*, II. *Corral Nocturne*, III. *Saturday Night Waltz*, IV. *Hoe-Down*. Plusieurs chansons traditionnels américains sont inclus dans la composition. Les sources ont été prises dans « Our Singing Country » de John A. et Alan Lomax et de la « Traditional Music of America » d'Ira Ford. Deux chants du livre de Lomax sont incorporés dans le premier épisode : « If he'd be a buckaroo by his trade » et « Sis Joe ». Les singularités rythmiques de « Sis Joe » offrent une matière riche pour le remaniement de la musique. Un air de quadrille intitulé « Bonyparte » fournit le thème principal de la *Hoe-Down*. Cependant, aucun emprunt à la musique folklorique n'a été fait pour la composition du *Corral Nocturne*.

Trois épisodes furent joués pour la première fois au cours d'un concert donné par le Boston Pops Orchestra sous la direction d'Arthur Fiedler le 28 mai 1943. La première de la suite dans son intégralité fut donnée au Stadium Concerts par le New York Philharmonic Symphony Orchestra dirigé par Alexander Smallens en juillet 1943.

ANMERKUNG

Das Ballet Russe de Monte Carlo beauftragte die Choreographin Agnes de Mille und den Komponisten Aaron Copland, gemeinsam an einem „Western-Ballett" für die Saison 1942-43 zu arbeiten. Mit dem ursprünglichen Untertitel *The Courting at Burnt Ranch* wurde *Rodeo* am 16. Oktober 1942 am Metropolitan Opera House (Bühnendekoration von Oliver Smith und Kostüme von Kermit Love) uraufgeführt.

Die Idee für das Ballett stammte von Agnes de Mille, die sie wie folgt beschrieb: „Im Südwesten Amerikas finden am Samstagnachmittag traditionell Rodeowettkämpfe statt. Auf den abgelegenen Ranches, in den Handelszentren und den Städten versammeln sich diejenigen, die ihre Geschicklichkeit mit dem Lasso und beim Reiten unter Beweis stellen wollen. Auf den abgelegeneren Ranches werden diese Rodeowettkämpfe oft vor einem Publikum aufgeführt, das nur aus einer Handvoll anderer Arbeiter, Frauen und den nächsten Nachbarn im Umkreis von ca. 100 km besteht. Der Vorstellung am Nachmittag folgt gewöhnlich am selben Abend ein Tanz im Haus auf der Ranch. Das Thema des Balletts ist einfach. Es handelt von den Schwierigkeiten, mit denen alle amerikanischen Frauen seit den frühesten Pioniertagen zu kämpfen haben und die sie zu jedem Zeitpunkt in der Geschichtes des Landes beschäftigen. Die Frage, wie man den richtigen Mann findet."

Die Musik wurde im Juni 1942 komponiert und im September desselben Jahres orchestriert. Der Komponist stellte später aus der Ballettpartitur eine Orchestersuite her, um diese konzertant unter dem Titel *Vier Tanzepisoden aus Rodeo:* I. *Buckaroo Holiday,* II. *Corral Nocturne,* III. *Saturday Night Waltz,* IV. *Hoe-Down* aufzuführen. In die Partitur wurden mehrere amerikanische Folksongs eingeflochten. Das Quellenmaterial stammt zum Teil aus „Our Singing Country" von John A. und Alan Lomax und aus „Traditional Music of America" von Ira Ford. Zwei Lieder aus dem Band von Lomax sind in die erste Episode eingearbeitet: „If he'd be a buckaroo by his trade" und „Sis Joe". Die rhythmischen Besonderheiten von „Sis Joe" boten reichhaltig Material zur Bearbeitung. Eine Squaredancemelodie mit dem Titel „Bonyparte" wurde zum Hauptthema in *Hoe-Down*. Für *Corral Nocturne* wurde allerdings kein Folklorematerial verwendet.

Drei Episoden wurden am 28. Mai 1943 vom Boston Pops Orchestra unter der Leitung von Arthur Fiedler konzertant uraufgeführt. Die ganze Suite wurde im Juli 1943 bei den Stadion-Konzerten vom New York Philharmonic Symphony Orchestra unter der Leitung von Alexander Smallens uraufgeführt.

BUCKAROO HOLIDAY
from
"RODEO"
DURATION
7 mins.
AARON COPLAND
Allegro con spirito 𝅗𝅥 = 112
I
Flutes
II & III
(Picc.I) (Picc.II)
Piccs. a 2
Oboes I & II
a2
Cor Anglais
Clarinets I & II
in B♭
a2
Bass Clarinet in B♭
Bassoons I & II
a 2
f marc. e stacc.
I & II
Horns in F
III & IV
f marc.
I
Trumpets in B♭
II & III
Trombones I & II
Trombone III
& Tuba
Timpani
Xylophone &
Glockenspiel
Percussion
Cymbal (hard stick)
Celeste
Piano & Harp
Allegro con spirito 𝅗𝅥 = 112
Violin I
Violin II
Viola
Violoncello
Contrabass
All rights reserved

1
Fl. I
Picc. I. II
Oboes I. II
C.A.
Clts. in B♭ I & II
B. Clt. in B♭
Bsns. I. II
I & II
Hns. in F
III & IV
I
Tpts. in B♭
II & III
Trombs. I & II
Tromb. III & Tuba
Timp.
Perc.
Cym.
B.D.
Piano
1
Vln. I
Vln. II
Vla.
'Cello
D.B.
a2
f
sf

2
Fl. I
Picc. I. II
Oboes I. II
C. A.
Clts. in B♭ I & II
a2
f marc.
B. Clt. in B♭
Bsns. I. II
I & II
Hns. in F
III & IV
a2
f marc.
f marc.
I
Tpts. in B♭
II & III
f marc.
f marc.
Trombs. I & II
f marc.
a2
f
Tromb. III & Tuba
Timp.
Perc.
8
Piano
2
Vln. I
f marc.
Vln. II
f marc.
Vla.
f marc.
div.
unis.
'Cello
f marc.
D. B.

3
Fl. I
Picc. I. II
Oboes I. II
C.A.
Clts. in B♭ I & II
B. Clt. in B♭
Bsns. I. II
I & II
Hns. in F
III & IV
I
Tpts. in B♭
II & III
Tromb s. I & II
Tromb. III & Tuba
Timp.
Perc.
Cym.
Piano
Vln. I
Vln. II
Vla.
'Cello
D.B.
a2
(a2)
f

4
Fl. I
Picc. I. II
a2
Oboes I. II
C.A.
Clts. in B♭ I & II
a2
B. Clt. in B♭
Bsns. I. II
I & II
Hns. in F
III & IV
I
Tpts. in B♭
II & III
Trombs. I & II
Tromb. III & Tuba
Timp.
Perc.
Piano
4
Vln. I
Vln. II
Vla.
div.
unis.
'Cello
D.B.

5 Meno mosso
Fl. I
a2
Picc. I. II
Take Flute II & III
Oboes I. II
C.A.
Clts. in B♭ I & II
B. Clt. in B♭
Bsns. I. II
con sord.
I & II
Hns in F
III & IV
Solo
con sord.
I
Tpts in B♭
II & III
Trombs I & II
Tromb III & Tuba
Timp.
Perc.
Piano
5 Meno mosso
Vln. I
Vln. II
Vla.
'Cello
D.B.

6
Fl. I
Flts. II. III
Oboes I. II
C. A.
Clts. in B♭ I & II
Soli
p with simple expression
B. Clt. in B♭
Bsns. I. II
pp
I & II
Hns in F
III & IV
I
Tpts in B♭
II & III
Trombs I & II
Tromb III & Tuba
Timp.
Perc.
Piano
6
con sord.
Vln. I
con sord.
Vln. II
con sord.
Vla.
con sord.
'Cello
D.B.

7
Fl. I
Flts. II. III
Oboes I. II
Solo
p with simple expression
C.A.
Clts. in B♭ I & II
Solo
B. Clt. in B♭
Bsns. I. II
p
I & II
Hns in F
III & IV
p
I
Tpts in B♭
II & III
p
Trombs I & II
p
Tromb III & Tuba
Timp.
Perc.
Piano
7
Vln. I
Vln. II
Vla.
'Cello
D.B.

8
Solo
Fl. I.
Flts. II. III
Oboes I. II
C.A.
Solo
Clts. in B♭ I & II
B. Clt. in B♭
Bsns. I. II
I & II
Hns. in F
III & IV
I
Tpts. in B♭
II & III
Trombs. I & II
Tromb. III & Tuba
Timp.
Perc.
Piano
8
Vln. I
Vln. II
Vla.
'Cello
D.B.

9
10 Poco più mosso
I
Flts.
II
Oboes I.II
a 2
Clts. in B♭
I & II
Soli
Bsn. I
Hns. in F
I & II
Tpt. II in B♭
Trombs.
I & II
9
10 Poco più mosso
senza sord.
Vln. I
senza sord.
Vln. II
poco a poco accel. e cresc. - - - (accel.) - - - -
Solo
I
Flts.
II
Oboes I.II
a 2
Clts. in B♭
I & II
poco a poco accel. e cresc. - - - (accel.) - - - -
pizz.
Vln. I
pizz.
Vln. II

11
Allegro (♩=𝅗𝅥) (𝅗𝅥=120)
I
Flts.
II
Oboes I.II
a 2
C.A
Clts. in B♭
I & II
B. Clt. in B♭
Bsn. I
secco
I & II
Hns. in F
III & IV
I
Tpts. in B♭
II
senza sord.
secco
Trombs.
I & II
con sord.
Tromb. III
& Tuba
Timp
Cym. (with brush)
Perc.
Piano
Vln. I
arco
Vln. II
Vla.
'Cello
D.B.
pizz.

12
Bsn. I
I
Tpts in B♭
II
Trombs. I & II
Cym.
sf
Perc.
Piano
sf
12
Vln. I
Vln. II
Vla.
sim.
'Cello
sf
D.B.
Solo
Fl. I
mp (with humor)
Solo
Clt. I in B♭
mp (with humor)
Bsn. I
senza sord.
I & II
Hns in F
III
mp
p senza sord.
I
Tpts. in B♭
II
Tromb. I
Wood-Block
Perc.
p
col legno
Vln. I
p pizz.
(col legno)
Vln. II
p
(arco)
'Cello
mp
(pizz.)
D.B.

13
Fl. I
sub. ff
Piccs. I.II
Oboes I.II
C.A.
Clts. in B♭ I & II
a 2
B. Clt. in B♭
Bsn. I
I & II
Hns. in F
III
cuivré
I
Tpts. in B♭
II & III
Tromb. I
Tromb. III & Tuba
Timp.
Xylo.
Wood-Block
Perc.
Snare Drum
rim-shot
Piano
Vln. I
(arco)
Vln. II
Vla.
p col legno
'Cello
D.B.

14
Fl I
Piccs. I.II
Oboes I.II
C.A.
a 2
Clts. in B♭ I & II
B.Clt. in B♭
Bsns. I.II
Hns. in F I & II
III & IV
Tpts. in B♭ I
II & III
Trombs. I & II
Tromb. III & Tuba
Timp.
Xylo.
Slap-stick
Perc.
B.D.
Piano
Vln. I
Vln. II
Vla.
'Cello
D.B.

15
Fl. I
Piccs. I II
Oboes I. II
C.A.
Clts. in B♭ I & II
B. Clt. in B♭
Bsns. I. II
I & II
Hns. in F
III & IV
I
Tpts. in B♭
II & III
Trombs. I & II
Tromb. III & Tuba
Timp.
Xylo.
Perc.
Piano
15
Vln. I
Vln. II
Vla.
'Cello
D. B.
a 2
(arco) div.
unis.

16
Fl. I
Piccs. I.II
Oboes I.II
a 2
C.A.
Clts. in B♭ I & II
B. Clt. in B♭
Bsns. I.II
I & II
Hns. in F
III & IV
I
Tpts. in B♭
II & III
Trombs. I & II
Tromb. III & Tuba
Timp.
Perc.
Piano
Vln. I
Vln. II
Vla.
'Cello
D.B.

Fl. I
Piccs. I. II
Oboes I. II
C.A.
Clts. in B♭ I & II
B. Clt. in B♭
Bsns. I. II
I & II
Hns. in F
III & IV
I
Tpts. in B♭
II & III
Trombs. I & II
Tromb. III & Tuba
Timp.
Perc.
Cym.
Piano
Vln. I
Vln. II
Vla.
'Cello
D.B.
a 2
sf
ff

17
Fl. I
Piccs. I.II
Oboes I.II
C.A.
Clts. in B♭ I & II
B. Clt. in B♭
Bsns. I.II
a 2
marc.
I & II
Hns. in F
III & IV
I
Tpts. in B♭
II & III
Trombs. I & II
a 2
Tromb. III & Tuba
Timp.
Perc.
8
Piano
17
Vln. I
8
div.
Vln. II
unis.
Vla.
'Cello
D. B.

18
Fl. I
Picc. I. II
Oboes I. II
C. A.
Clts. in B♭ I & II
B. Clt. in B♭
Bsns. I. II
I & II
Hns. in F
III
I
Tpts. in B♭
II & III
Trombs. I & II
Tromb. III & Tuba
Timp.
Perc.
Piano
Vln. I
Vln. II
Vla.
'Cello
D.B.
ff
a2
f
a 2

19
Fl.I
Picc.I.II
Oboes I.II
C.A.
Clts.in B♭ I & II
B.Clt.in B♭
Bsns.I.II
I & II
Hns.in F
III & IV
I
Tpts.in B♭
II & III
Trombs. I & II
Tromb.III & Tuba
Timp.
Perc.
Piano
Vln.I
Vln.II
Vla
'Cello
D.B.
a2
ff
div.
unis.
8

20
L'istesso tempo
Fl. I
Picc. I. II
Oboes I. II
C.A.
Clts. in B♭ I & II
B. Clt. in B♭
Bsns. I. II
I Solo
I & II
Hns. in F
III & IV
I
Tpts. in B♭
II & III
Tromb. I & II
Tromb. III & Tuba
Timp.
Perc.
B.D.
Piano
20
L'istesso tempo
Vln. I
Vln. II
Vla
'Cello
D. B.
Solo
secco
poco

21
Bsn. I
I & II
Hns. in F
III
Tromb. I
Vln. I
Vln. II
Vla.
D.B.
p
mf
p secco
Solo (with humor)
mp
at the frog
secco p
sim.
(Solo)
sf
p
sfmf
22
Clt. I. in B♭
Solo
(Perky)
pizz.

23
Fl. I
Picc. I.
Oboes I. II
C.A.
Cl.ts in B♭ I & II
B. Cl.t. in B♭
Bsns. I. II
I & II
Hns. in F
III & IV
I
Tpts. in B♭
II & III
Trombs. I & II
Tromb. III & Tuba
Timp.
Perc.
Piano
Vln. I
Vln. II
Vla
'Cello
D.B.
Solo
a2
p secco
secco
(with humor)
Snare Dr.
With brush
pizz.
arco
unis.

Clts. in B♭ I & II
B. Clt. in B♭
Bsns. I. II
Trpt. I. in B♭
Perc.
S.D.
sf
Vln. I
Vln. II
Vla.
'Cello
D.B.
24
Oboe I
Solo
mf (perky)
B. Clt. in B♭
Bsn. I.
Tpt. I. in B♭
p
Perc.
S.D.
pp
24
Vln. I
arco
p
Vln. II
arco
p
Vla.
arco
p
'Cello
D.B.

25
Fl.I
Picc.I
Oboe I
C.A.
Clts.in B♭ I & II
B.Clt.in B♭
Bsn. I
I & II
Hns.in F
III & IV
I
Tpts.in B♭
II & III
Trombs I & II
Tromb. III & Tuba
Timp.
Perc.
Celesta
Piano
HARP
Vln.I
Vln.II
Vla.
'Cello
D.B.
Solo
secco
con sord.
div.

26
Fl. I
Picc. I
Oboe I
C. A.
Clt. II in B♭
B. Clt. in B♭
Bsn. I
I & II
Hns. in F
III & IV
I
Tpts. in B♭
II & III
Trombs I & II
Tromb. III & Tuba
Timp.
Perc.
Celesta
Harp
Solo
Vln. I
Vln. II
Vla.
'Cello
D.B.

27
Fl. I
Picc. I
Oboe I
C.A.
Clts. in B♭ I & II
Solo
mf
B. Clt. in B♭
Bsn. I
I & II
Hns. in F
III & IV
I
Tpts. in B♭
II
(senza sord.)
p
Tromb. I
p (senza sord.)
Trom. III & Tuba
Timp.
Perc.
Celesta
Harp
27
Vln. I
secco
mf
col legno
p
Vln. II
unis. pizz.
p
Vla.
unis.
secco mf
'Cello
mf secco
D.B.

28
Solo
Fl. I
Piccs. I. II
Solo
Oboe I
C. A.
Clt. I in B♭
B. Clt. in B♭
Solo
Bsn. I
con sord.
I & II
Hns. in F
con sord.
III & IV
(senza sord.)
I
Tpts. in B♭
II
senza sord.
senza sord.
senza sord.
Tromb. I
Tromb. III & Tuba
Timp.
Wood Bk.
Cym.
with brush
Piano
modo ordinario
col legno
28
Vln. I
Vln. II
Vla.
col legno
'Cello
secco
D.B.
pizz.

Fl. I
Piccs. I. II
Oboes I. II
C.A.
Clt. I in B♭
B. Clt. in B♭
Bsn. I
I & II
Hns. in F
III & IV
I
Tpts. in B♭
II
Trombs. I & II
Tromb. III & Tuba
Timp.
Cym.
Piano
Vln. I
Vln. II
Vla.
'Cello
D.B.
Solo
con sord.
modo ordin.
arco
modo ordin.

29
Fl. I
Piccs. I.II
Oboes I.II
C. A.
Clts. in B♭ I & II
B.Clt. in B♭
Bsns. I.II
I & II
Hns. in F
III & IV
I
Tpts. in B♭
II & III
Trombs. I & II
Tromb. III & Tuba
Timp.
Perc.
Piano
Vln. I
Vln. II
Vla.
'Cello
D.B.
sub. ff
sf
a 2
ff
senza sord. a 2
(II senza sord.)
mf
29

Fl. I
Piccs. I. II
Oboes I. II
C.A.
Clts. in B♭ I & II
B.Clt. in B♭
Bsns. I. II
I & II
Hns. in F
III & IV
I
Tpts. in B♭
II & III
Trombs. I & II
Tromb. III & Tuba
Timp.
Perc.
Piano
Vln. I
Vln. II
Vla.
'Cello
D.B.
a 2
sf

30
Fl. I
Piccs. I. II
a 2
Oboes I. II
C.A.
a 2
Soli
Clts. in B♭ I & II
f
sf
mf
B. Clt. in B♭
a 2
Bsns. I. II
con sord.
a 2
I & II
Hns. in F
III & IV
a 2
mf
p
I
Tpts. in B♭
II & III
a 2
a 2
Trombs. I & II
Tromb. III & Tuba
Timp.
Perc.
Harp
mf
p
30
1st desk (2 Soli)—non sentimental
div.
div.
Vln. I
f
sf
mp
Vln. II
mf
p
Vla.
mf
p
'Cello
arco
f
sfp
D.B.
f
sfp

31
Solo
mp
Fl. I
Piccs. I.II
Soli
p
Solo
mp
Oboes I.II
C.A.
Clts. in B♭ I & II
B. Clt. in B♭
pp
Bsn. I
I & II
Hns. in F
III & IV
p
I
Tpts. in B♭
II
con sord.
pp
Trombs. I & II
Tromb. III & Tuba
Timp.
Glock.
(actual sound)
p
Glock.
Perc.
Harp
31
gracefully
unis.
Tutti
mp
Vln. I
Vln. II
Vla.
'Cello
D. B.

32
Fl. I
Piccs. I. II
Oboe I
C.A.
Clts. in B♭ I & II
B.Clt. in B♭
Bsn. I
I & II Hns. in F III & IV
I Tpts. in B♭ II
Trombs. I & II
Tromb. III & Tuba
Timp.
Glock.
Perc.
Harp
32
Vln. I
Vln. II
Vla.
'Cello
D.B.

33
Fl. I
Picc. I
Oboe I
C.A.
Clts. in B♭ I & II
B. Clt. in B♭
Bsn. I
I & II Hns. in F III & IV
I Tpts. in B♭ II
Trombs. I & II
Tromb. III & Tuba
Timp.
Glock.
Perc.
Harp
Vln. I
Vln. II
Vla.
'Cello
D.B.
Solo
mp
p
mf
pp
33

34
Solo
Fl. I
Picc. I
Oboe I
C.A.
Clt. I in B♭
B.Clt. in B♭
Bsn. I
senza sord.
I & II
Hns. in F
III
senza sord.
Solo
I
Tpts. in B♭
II
Trombs. I & II
Tromb. III & Tuba
Timp.
Glock.
Perc.
Harp
34
Vln. I
Vln. II
Vla.
'Cello
D.B.

35
I & II
Hns. in F
III
senza sord.
Tpt. II in B♭
mf
35
Vln. I
Vln. II
Vla.
'Cello
D.B.
sf
I & II
Hns. in F
III & IV
f
cresc.
I
Tpts. in B♭
II & III
Trombs. I & II
a 2
Tromb. III & Tuba
detaché

36
Fl. I
Picc. I.II
a 2
Oboes I.II
C. A.
Clts. in B♭ I & II
B. Clt. in B♭
Bsns. I.II
I & II
Hns. in F
III & IV
I
Tpts. in B♭
II & III
Trombs. I & II
Tromb. III & Tuba
Timp.
Cym.
(2 Plates)
let it vibrate
Piano
Vln. I
Vln. II
Vla.
'Cello
D.B.

Fl. I
Picc. I.II
Oboes I.II
C. A.
Clts. in B♭ I & II
B. Clt. in B♭
Bsns. I.II
I & II
Hns. in F
III & IV
I
Tpts. in B♭
II & III
Trombs. I & II
Tromb. III & Tuba
Timp.
Perc.
Piano
Vln. I
Vln. II
Vla.
'Cello
D. B.
a 2

37
Fl. I
Picc. I.II
Oboes I.II
C. A.
Clts. in B♭ I & II
B. Clt. in B♭
Bsns. I.II
I & II
Hns. in F
III & IV
I
Tpts. in B♭
II & III
Trombs. I & II
Tromb. III & Tuba
Timp.
Xylo.
Snare Drum
B. D.
Piano
Vln. I
Vln. II
Vla.
'Cello
D. B.
a 2
cuivre
cuivré

38
Fl. I
Picc. I.II
Oboes I.II
C.A.
Clts. in B♭ I & II
B.Clt. in B♭
Bsns. I.II
I & II
Hns. in F
III & IV
I
Tpts. in B♭
II & III
Trombs. I & II
Tromb. III & Tuba
Timp.
Xylo.
Slap stick
B.D.
38
Piano
marc.
Vln. I
Vln. II
Vla.
'Cello
D. B.

Fl. I
Picc. I. II
Oboes I. II
C. A.
Clts. in B♭ I & II
B. Clt. in B♭
Bsns. I. II
I & II
Hns. in F
III & IV
I
Tpts. in B♭
II & III
Tromb. I & II
Tromb. III & Tuba
Timp.
Snare Drum
Piano
Vln. I
Vln. II
Vla.
'Cello
D. B.
a 2
ff
ff marc.
sff

39
Fl. I
Picc. I. II
Oboes I. II
C. A.
Clts. in B♭ I & II
B. Clt. in B♭
Bsns. I. II
I & II Hns. in F III & IV
I Tpts. in B♭ II & III
8va ad lib.
a 2
Trombs. I & II
Tromb. III & Tuba
Timp.
rim-shot
Snare Dr
Slap stick B. D.
Piano
39
Vln. I
Vln. II
Vla.
'Cello
D. B.

40
Fl. I
Picc. I.II
Oboes I.II
C. A.
Clts. in B♭ I & II
B. Clt. in B♭
Bsns. I.II
a 2
I & II
Hns. in F
III & IV
I
Tpts. in B♭
II & III
Trombs. I & II
Tromb. III & Tuba
Timp.
Perc.
Piano
40
Vln. I
Vln. II
Vla.
'Cello
D. B.

41
Silent (short)
Fl. I
Picc. I. II
Oboes. I.II
C.A.
Clts. in B♭ I & II
B.Clt. in B♭
Bsns. I. II
a 2
cuivré
I & II
Hns. in F
III & IV
I
Tpts. in B♭
II & III
Trombs. I & II
Tromb. III & Tuba
Timp.
rim-shot
Sn. Dr.
Slap stick
Piano
Vln. I
Vln. II
Vla.
'Cello
D.B.

42
Fl. I
Picc. I. II
Oboes. I.II
C.A.
Clts. in B♭ I & II
B.Clt. in B♭
Bsns. I.II
I & II
Hns. in F
III & IV
I
Tpts. in B♭
II & III
Trombs. I & II
Tromb. III & Tuba
Timp.
Perc.
B.D.
secco
Piano
Vln. I
Vln. II
Vla.
'Cello
D.B.
a 2
stacc.
42

Fl. I
Picc. I. II
Oboes I. II
C. A.
Clts. in B♭ I & II
B. Clt. in B♭
e pesante
a 2
pesante
Bsns. I. II
I & II
Hns. in F
III & IV
I
Tpts. in B♭
II & III
a 2
Trombs. I & II
Tromb. III & Tuba
Timp.
Perc.
8
Piano
Vln. I
Vln. II
Vla.
'Cello
D.B.

Fl. I
Picc. I. II
Oboes I. II
C.A.
Clts. in B♭ I & II
B. Clt. in B♭
a 2
Bsns. I. II
I & II
Hns. in F
III & IV
I
Tpts. in B♭
II & III
a 2
Trombs. I & II
Tromb. III & Tuba
Timp.
Perc.
Piano
Vln. I
Vln. II
Via.
'Cello
D.B.

43
Broadly
Fl. I
Picc. I. II
a 2
Oboes I. II
C. A.
Clts. in B♭ I & II
B. Clt. in B♭
Bsns. I. II
I & II
Hns. in F
III & IV
I
Tpts. in B♭
II & III
Trombs. I & II
Tromb. III & Tuba
Timp.
Tria.
2 plates
Cym. & B.D.
Piano
43
Broadly
Vln. I
Vln. II
Vla.
'Cello
D. B.

Sub. a tempo
Fl. I
Picc. I. II
a 2
Oboes I.II
C.A.
Clts. in B♭ I & II
B.Clt. in B♭
Bsns. I.II
I & II
Hns. in F
III & IV
I
Tpts. in B♭
II & III
Trombs. I & II
Tromb. III & Tuba
Timp.
Snare Dr.
Cym. & B.D.
(hard stick)
B.D.
Piano
8ba.
Sub. a tempo
Vln. I
Vln. II
Vla.
'Cello
D.B.
marc.

CORRAL NOCTURNE
from
"RODEO"

AARON COPLAND

rit. - - - a tempo
Fl.
Oboe
I
Clts. in B♭
II
Bsn.
Solo
senza sord.
Hns. in F
senza sord.
I
Tpts. in B♭
II
senza sord.
con sord.
con sord.
senza sord.
Tromb.
Celesta
Harp
rit. - - - a tempo
1st Desk (div.)
Tutti (unis.)
Vln. I
Vln. II
Vla.
pizz.
arco
'Cello
pizz.
arco
pizz.
Bass
pizz.

2
Fl.
Solo
p
poco cresc.
Oboe
Solo
p
poco cresc.
I
Clts.in B♭
II
p
poco cresc.
Bsn.
poco cresc.
Hns.in F
p
poco cresc.
I
Tpts.in B♭
II
senza sord.
p
poco cresc.
Tromb.
p
poco cresc.
Celesta
p
Harp
p
2
Vln.I
p
poco cresc.
Vln.II
p
poco cresc.
Vla.
(unis.)
div.a 3
p
poco cresc.
'Cello
arco
p
poco cresc.
Bass
arco
p
poco cresc.

3 Tempo I
Fl.
Oboe
Solo
I
Clts. in B♭
II
Bsn.
Hns in F
I
Tpts. in B♭
II
senza sord.
Tromb.
Celesta
Harp
3 Tempo I
Vln. I
Vln. II
(unis.)
Vla.
'Cello
pizz
arco
Bass
pizz
arco

Solo
p
mp
4
Fl.
Oboe
Solo
p<mf
I
Clts.in B♭
II
Solo
p
Solo
Bsn.
p<mf
Hns.in F
I
Tpts.in B♭
II
Tromb.
Celesta
Harp
4
Vln.I
p
Vln.II
p
Vla.
p
arco
'Cello
p
arco
Bass
p

5
Fl.
Oboe
Solo
I
Clts.in B♭
II
Bsn.
Hns.in F
I
Tpts.in B♭
II
Tromb.
Celesta
Harp
5
Vln.I
Vln.II
Vla.
'Cello
Bass

Solo
Fl.
Oboe
I
Clts.in B♭
II
Bsn.
Hns.in F
I
Tpts.in B♭
II
Tromb.
Celesta
Harp
Vln.I
Vln.II
div.a 3
Vla.
'Cello
Bass

6
rit.molto
Fl.
pp
Oboe
pp
I
Clts.in B♭
II
Bsn.
pp
Hns.in F
p
con sord.
pp
ppp
Solo con sord.
I
Tpts.in B♭
II
pp
con sord.
pp
ppp
con sord.
Tromb.
p
pp
ppp
Celesta
Harp
6
div.
unis.
rit.molto
Vln.I
pp
ppp
Vln.II
pp
ppp
unis.
Vla.
pp
ppp
pizz. arco
'Cello
pp
pizz.
arco
pizz.
arco
ppp
pizz. arco
Bass
pp
pizz.
arco
pizz.
arco
ppp

SATURDAY NIGHT WALTZ
from
"RODEO"

DURATION 4 mins.

AARON COPLAND

I Broader

dim. e rit. poco a poco

Flt.

Oboe

Solo

mf simply

I

Clts. in B♭

II

B. Clt. in B♭

Bsn.

I

Hns. in F

II

meno f

I

Tpts. in B♭

II

Tromb.

Harp

I Broader

dim. e rit. poco a poco

Vln. I

Vln. II

Vla.

'Cello

arco

Bass

2 Slow Waltz (♩ = 72)
Oboe
I
Cls. in B♭
II
B. Clt. in B♭
Harp
2 Slow Waltz (♩ = 72)
Vln. I
Cello
Solo
3
Flt.
Oboe
I
Cls. in B♭
II
B. Clt. in B♭
I
Hns. in F
II
Harp
3
Vln. I
Vln. II
Vla.
'Cello

4
Solo
Flt.
Oboe
I
Clts. in B♭
II
B. Clt. in B♭
p
Harp
4
Vln. I
Vln. II
Vla.
Cello
Flt.
B. Clt. in B♭
p
I
Hns. in F
II
Vln. I
mp
Vln. II
Vla.
'Cello

5
Solo
Flt.
mp
Oboe
mf
I
Clts. in B♭
II
mp
mp
B. Clt. in B♭
Bsn.
I
Hns. in F
II
I
pts. in B♭
II
Tromb.
Harp
mp
5
Vln. I
mf
Vln. II
mp
Vla.
'Cello

Solo
Flt.
p
Oboe
I
Clts. in B♭
II
B.Clt. in B♭
I
Hns. in F
II
Harp
Vln. I
Vln. II
Vla.
'Cello
6
Doppio movimento (𝅗𝅥 = ♩)
poco rit.
Solo
mp
Bsn.
pp

7 Meno mosso
Solo
p lazily
Solo
p lazily
p
p
p
con sord
p
7 Meno mosso
mp espress.
8
p
8
p
Flt.
I
Clts. in B♭
II
B. Clt. in B♭
Bsn.
Tromb.
Vln. I
Vln. II
Vla.
'Cello

Flt.
I
Clts. in B♭
II
B. Clt. in B♭
Bsn.
p
Tromb.
Vln. I
Vln. II
Vla.
'Cello
9
Flt.
I
Clts. in B♭
II
B. Clt. in B♭
Bsn.
Tromb.
9
Vln. I
pp
p
Vln. II
mf
Vla.
'Cello

10 Tempo I
Oboe
Clt. I in B♭
I
Hns. in F
II
mf
f
10 Tempo I
Vln. I
Vln. II
Vla.
'Cello
11
Solo
Flt.
Oboe
I
Tpts. in B♭
II
B. Clt. in B♭
I
Hns. in F
II
Harp
11
Vln. I
Vln. II
Vla.
'Cello

rit.
Flt.
Oboe
I
Clts. in B♭
II
B. Clt. in B♭
Bsn.
I
Hns. in F
II
I
Tpts. in B♭
II
Tromb.
Harp
rit.
Vln. I
Vln. II
div.
Vla.
'Cello

HOE-DOWN
from
"RODEO"

AARON COPLAND

I
Picc.
Flts. I & II
a 2
Oboes I & II
a 2
f
C. A.
Clts. I & II in B♭
a 2
f
Bass Clt. in B♭
Bsns. I & II
a 2
I & II
Hns. in F
III & IV
I
Tpts. in B♭
f
II & III
Tromb. I
B. Tromb. & Tuba
Timp.
f
S. D.
I
div.
Vln. I
f
Vln. II
f
marc.
Vla.
f
marc.
'Cello
marc.
Bass

2
Picc.
Flts. I & II
Oboes I & II
C. A.
Clts. I & II in B♭
Bass Clt. in B♭
Bsns. I & II
I & II
Hns. in F
III & IV
I
Tpts. in B♭
II & III
Tromb. I
B. Tromb. & Tuba
Timp.
W. B.
S. D.
Cym.
Piano
Vln. I
Vln. II
Vla.
'Cello
Bass
ff
a 2
f
senza sord.
hard stick
p
mf
sec.
unis
pizz.
(pizz.)

3
sec.
Bsn. I
mf
W. B.
Piano
f
3
pizz.
arco
pizz.
Vln. I
pizz.
arco
pizz.
Vln. II
pizz.
Vla.
mf sec.
'Cello
sub f
Bass
Bsn. I
W. B.
Piano
arco
pizz.
arco
Vln. I
arco
pizz.
arco
Vln. II
Vla.
'Cello
Bass

4
5
Picc.
Flts. I & II
a 2
f
Oboes I & II
C.A.
Clts. I & II in B♭
Bass Clt. in B♭
Bsn. I
I & II
Hns. in F
III & IV
I
Tpts. in B♭
II
Trombs. I & II
B. Tromb. & Tuba
Xylo.
W. B.
Cym.
hard stick
Piano
Vln. I
Vln. II
Vla.
'Cello
Bass

Picc.
Flts. I & II
a 2
sf
Oboes I & II
a 2
sf
C. A.
Clts. I & II in B♭
a 2
Bass Clt. in B♭
sf
Bsn. I
sf
I & II
Hns. in F
III & IV
I
Tpts. in B♭
II
sf
Trombs. I & II
B. Tromb. & Tuba
Xylo.
sf
Cym.
f
hard stick
Vln. I
Vln. II
Vla.
'Cello
Bass

6
a 2
f non legato
Oboes I & II
Clts I & II in B♭
a 2
f non legato
Hns I & II in F
f
Trombs I & II
f
6
Vln. I
Vln. II
Vla.
'Cello
Bass
a 2
Oboes I & II
Clts I & II in B♭
a2
Hns I & II in F
Trombs I & II
Vln. I
Vln. II
Vla.
'Cello
Bass

7
Picc.
Flts. I & II
a 2
Oboes I & II
a 2
C. A.
Clts. I & II in B♭
a 2
Bass Clt. in B♭
Bsn. I
I & II
Hns. in F
III & IV
I
Tpts. in B♭
II & III
Trombs. I & II
B. Tromb. & Tuba
Xylo.
Cym.
hard stick
7
Vln. I
Vln. II
Vla.
'Cello
Bass

8
Picc.
a2
Flts. I & II
sf
a2
Oboes I & II
sf
C.A.
a2
Clts. I & II in B♭
Bass Clt. in B♭
sf
Bsn. I
sf
I & II
Hns. in F
III & IV
mf
I
Tpts. in B♭
II
sf
Trombs. I & II
B.Tromb. & Tuba
Timp.
p
Xylo.
sf
8
Vln. I
Vln. II
Vla.
'Cello
Bass
sf
mf
arco

9
Picc.
Flts. I & II
a 2
mp
ff
Oboes I & II
C. A.
Clts. I & II in B♭
Bass Clt. in B♭
Bsns. I & II
I & II
Hns. in F
III & IV
I
Tpts. in B♭
II & III
Trombs. I & II
B.Tromb. & Tuba
Timp.
Xylo.
Tria.
Vln. I
Vln. II
Vla.
'Cello
Bass
p
fff
pizz.

Picc.
a2
Flts. I & II
a2
Oboes I & II
C.A.
a2
Clts. I & II in B♭
Bass Clt. in B♭
Bsns I & II
I & II
Hns. in F
III & IV
I
Tpts. in B♭
II & III
Trombs. I & II
B.Tromb. & Tuba
Timp.
Tria.
Vln. I
Vln. II
Vla.
'Cello
Bass

10
Picc.
Flts. I & II
a2
Oboes I & II
C.A.
Clts. I & II in B♭
Bass Clt. in B♭
Bsns. I
I & II
Hns. in F
III & IV
I
Tpts. in B♭
II
Trombs. I & II
B.Tromb. & Tuba
Xylo.
Hard stick
Cym.
Vln. I
Vln. II
Vla.
arco.
'Cello
Bass

11
Picc.
Flts. I & II
Oboes I & II
C.A.
Clts. I & II in B♭
Bass Clt. in B♭
Bsns. I
I & II
Hns. in F
III & IV
I
Tpts. in B♭
II
Trombs. I & II
B. Tromb. & Tuba
Xylo.
Cym.
Vln. I
Vln. II
Vla.
'Cello
Bass
a2
sf
f

Picc.
Flts. I & II
Oboes I & II
C.A.
Clts. I & II in B♭
Bass Clt. in B♭
Bsns. I & II
I & II
Hns. in F
III & IV
I
Tpts. in B♭
II & III
Tromb. I
B. Tromb. & Tuba
Timp.
Xylo.
S.D.
Cym.
Vln. I
Vln. II
Vla.
'Cello
Bass
a2
sf
cresc.
fff
ff
f
mf cresc.
dim. molto
sff
arco.

12
Picc.
Flts. I & II
Oboes I & II
C.A.
Clts. I & II in B♭
Bass Clt. in B♭
Bsns. I & II
I & II
Hns. in F
III & IV
I
Tpts. in B♭
II & III
Trombs. I & II
B. Tromb. & Tuba
Timp.
S.D.
Vln. I
Vln. II
Vla.
'Cello
Bass
dim. molto
p
f
(a2)
Solo
rim shot
pizz.
3

13
Solo
Oboe I
mf non legato
Clts. I & II in B♭
p
Bsns. I & II
I
Tpts. in B♭
II
Trombs. I & II
a2
B. Tromb & Tuba
rim
S. D.
rim
13
arco
div. pizz.
Vln. I
f
p
Vln. II
f
div. pizz.
Vla.
f
p
arco
'Cello
arco
Bass
Oboe I
mf Solo
Clts. I & II in B♭
Bass Clt. in B♭
p
Bsn. I
p
(arco)
Solo Vln.
Vln. I (div.)
mf
Vla. (div.)

14
Picc.
Flts. I & II
Solo
Oboe I
mf
C.A.
Clt. I in B♭
Bass Clt. in B♭
a 2
Bsns. I & II
f
I & II
Hns. in F
III & IV
I
Tpts. in B♭
II
f
Trombs. I & II
B. Tromb. & Tuba
Timp.
rim shot
S.D.
14
unis. arco.
Vln. I
pizz..
arco
Vln. II
unis. arco
Vla. (div.)
pizz.
arco
'Cello
pizz.
arco
Bass

15
Picc.
Flt. I
Oboes I & II
C.A.
Clts. I & II in B♭
Bass Clt. in B♭
Bsns. I & II
a2
I & II
Hns. in F
III & IV
I
Tpts. in B♭
II
Trombs. I & II
B. Tromb. & Tuba
Timp.
S.D.
Piano
15
Vln. I
Vln. II
Vla.
'Cello
Bass
ff
f
f vigoroso
arco

16
Picc.
Flt. I
oboes I & II
a2
stacc.
ff
C. A.
ts. I & II in B♭
Bass Clt. in B♭
sns. I & II
I & II
Hns. in F
III & IV
I
pts. in B♭
II
Trombs. I & II
Tromb. & Tuba
Timp.
Piano
Vln. I
Vln. II
Vla.
'Cello
Bass
sf

Picc.
ff
Flts. I & II
a 2
Oboes I & II
a 2
C.A.
Clts. I & II in B♭
a 2
Bass Clt. in B♭
Bsns. I & II
I & II
Hns. in F
III & IV
a 2
I
Tpts. in B♭
II & III
Trombs. I & II
a 2
B. Tromb. & Tuba
Timp.
Vln. I
Vln. II
Vla.
'Cello
Bass

17
Picc.
Flts. I & II
Oboes I & II
C. A.
Clts. I & II in B♭
Bass Clt. in B♭
Bsns. I & II
I & II
Hns. in F
III & IV
I
Tpts. in B♭
II & III
Trombs. I & II
B. Tromb. & Tuba
Timp.
S.D.
W.B.
Cym.
B.D.
Piano
Vln. I
Vln. II
Vla.
'Cello
Bass
a2
a 2
fff
ff
sf
mf
mp
f
SD.
W.B.
rubato
(arco)
pizz.
8

18
Bsn. I
Hns. in F I & II
Tromb. I
Solo
mf
W. B.
Piano
18
Vln. I
Vln. II
Vla.
'Cello
Bass
p
rit. molto
Clts. I & II in B♭
Celesta
(pizz.)
arco

19
Picc.
Clts. I & II
a 2
Oboes I & II
C. A.
Clts. I & II in B♭
Bass Clt. in B♭
Bsn. I
I & II
Hns. in F
III & IV
I
Tpts. in B♭
II
Trombs. I & II
B. Tromb. & Tuba
Xylo.
Cym.
(hard stick)
Vln. I
Vln. II
Vla.
'Cello
Bass

Picc.
Flts. I & II
Oboes I & II
C.A.
Clts. I & II in B♭
Bass Clt. in B♭
Bsns. I & II
I & II
Hns. in F
III & IV
I
Tpts. in B♭
II
Trombs. I & II
B.Tromb. & Tuba
Xylo.
Vln. I
Vln. II
Vla.
'Cello
Bass

20
Picc.
a2
Flts. I & II
ff
Oboes I & II
C.A.
Clts. I & II in B♭
Bass Clt. in B♭
Bsns. I & II
I & II
Hns. in F
III & IV
I
Tpts. in B♭
II & III
Trombs. I & II
a 2
B. Tromb. & Tuba
Timp.
Tria.
Vln. I
fff
Vln. II
Vla.
'Cello
pizz.
Bass

21
Picc.
Flts. I & II
a2
Oboes I & II
C.A.
Clts. I & II in B♭
a 2
Bass Clt. in B♭
Bsn. I
I & II
Hns. in F
III & IV
I
Tpts. in B♭
II & III
Trombs. I & II
B. Tromb. & Tuba
Timp.
Xylo.
Tria. Cym.
Vln. I
Vln. II
Vla.
'Cello
arco.
Bass

22
Picc.
Flts. I & II
Oboes I & II
C.A.
Clts. I & II in B♭
Bass Clt. in B♭
Bsns. I & II
I & II
Hns. in F
III & IV
I
Tpts. in B♭
II & III
Trombs. I & II
B. Tromb. & Tuba
Xylo.
Tria. Cym.
Piano
22
Vln. I
Vln. II
Vla.
'Cello
Bass
a2
cresc.
ff
f
p

Picc.
Flts. I & II
Oboes I & II
C.A.
Clts. I & II in B♭
Bass Clt. in B♭
Bsns. I & II
I & II
Hns. in F
III & IV
I
Tpts. in B♭
II & III
Trombs. I & II
B. Tromb. & Tuba
Timp.
Xylo.
Tria. Cym. B.D.
Piano
Vln. I
Vln. II
Vla.
'Cello
Bass
cuivré
a2
B.D.
arco

APPALACHIAN SPRING SUITE

Instrumentation

2 Flutes
2 Oboes
2 Clarinets in A and B♭
2 Bassoons
2 Horns in F
2 Trumpets in B♭
2 Trombones
Timpani
Percussion
xylophone, snare drum, bass drum, cymbals,
tabor (long drum), snare drum, wood block,
claves, glockenspiel, triangle
Harp
Piano
Strings

Duration: c. 20 minutes

NOTE

Appalachian Spring was composed in 1943-44 as a ballet for Martha Graham on a commission from the Elizabeth Sprague Coolidge Foundation. It was first performed by Martha Graham and her company at the Coolidge Festival in the Library of Congress, Washington DC, on 30 October, 1944.

The original scoring called for a chamber ensemble of thirteen instruments. The present arrangement for symphony orchestra was made by the composer in the spring of 1945. It is a condensed version of the ballet, retaining all essential features but omitting those sections in which the interest is primarily choreographic.

The action of the ballet concerns "a pioneer celebration in spring around a newly-built farmhouse in the Pennsylvania hills in the early part of the last century. The bride-to-be and the young farmer-husband enact the emotions, joyful and apprehensive, their new domestic partnership invites. An older neighbour suggests now and then the rocky confidence of experience. A revivalist and his followers remind the new householders of the strange and terrible aspects of human fate. At the end the couple are left quiet and strong in their new house."

In 1945 *Appalachian Spring* received the Pulitzer Prize for music as well as the award of the Music Critics Circle of New York for the outstanding theatrical work of the season 1944-45.

NOTE

Appalachian Spring qui fut composé en 1943-44 comme ballet pour Martha Graham, sur la commande de l'Elizabeth Sprague Coolidge Foundation, a été représenté pour la première fois par Martha Graham et sa compagnie au Coolidge Festival dans la Bibliothèque du Congrès à Washington DC, le 30 octobre 1944.

L'arrangement original nécessitait un ensemble de chambre de treize instruments. L'arrangement ici reproduit, pour orchestre symphonique, a été réalisé par le compositeur au printemps 1945. C'est une version condensée du ballet, qui en retient toutes les caractéristiques essentielles mais omet les sections dont l'intérêt est principalement chorégraphique.

L'argument du ballet est « une fête de pionniers qui se déroule au printemps, autour d'une ferme récemment construite dans les collines de Pennsylvanie, au début du siècle dernier. La future épouse et son futur époux, le jeune fermier, nous montrent leurs émotions, leur joie et leur appréhension, que leur inspire leur future vie à deux. Un voisin plus âgé suggère, de temps en temps, la confiance qui vient avec l'expérience. Un « revivaliste » et ses adeptes rappellent au nouveau couple les étranges et terribles aspects de la destinée humaine. A la fin du ballet le couple est laissé, tranquille et solide, dans sa nouvelle demeure ».

En 1945 *Appalachian Spring* reçoit le Pulitzer Prize pour la musique, ainsi que le prix du Music Critics Circle de New York pour le travail théâtral extraordinaire accompli au cours de la saison 1944-45.

ANMERKUNG

Appalachian Spring wurde 1943-44 als Ballett für Martha Graham im Auftrag der Elizabeth-Sprague-Coolidge-Stiftung komponiert und am 30. Oktober 1944 von Martha Graham und ihrer Compagnie auf dem Coolidge-Festival in der Library of Congress, Washington DC, uraufgeführt.

In der Originalpartitur war ein Kammerorchester mit 13 Instrumenten vorgesehen. Die heutige Fassung für Sinfonieorchester wurde vom Komponisten im Frühjahr 1945 hergestellt. Hierbei handelt es sich um eine verkürzte Version des Balletts, die alle wichtigen Elemente beibehält, aber diejenigen Teile ausläßt, die hauptsächlich von choreographischem Interesse sind.

Das Thema des Balletts ist „eine Pionierfeier im Frühjahr anläßlich eines neugebauten Farmhauses in den Bergen von Pennsylvania in der ersten Hälfte des letzten Jahrhunderts. Die zukünftige Braut und der junge Bräutigam-Farmer drücken die gemischten Gefühle aus, die sie in Bezug auf ihre Ehe und das gemeinsame Leben haben. Ein älterer Nachbar weist auf die Bedeutung von Erfahrung im Leben hin. Ein Führer der Erweckungsbewegung und seine Anhänger erinnern das junge Paar an die seltsamen und schrecklichen Fügungen des menschlichen Schicksals. Am Schluß wird das Paar allein, aber gestärkt im neuen Haus zurückgelassen."

Appalachian Spring erhielt 1945 den Pulitzer-Preis für Musik und den Preis des New Yorker Music Critics Circle (Musikkritikerkreis) als überragende Bühnenarbeit in der Saison 1944-45.

APPALACHIAN SPRING

Ballet for Martha

Aaron Copland
(1943-1944)

2 Moving forward
I.
Fl.
II.
Solo
mf cant.
Cl. I (in A)
Solo
Fg. I. II
I. Solo
mf
Cor. (F) I. II
I. con sord.
Tr. (B♭) I. II
con sord.
I. Solo
mf
Moving forward
Arpa
Vl. I
Vln. 8va Solo
Vl. II
Vla.
Vc.
div.
3 rit.
Fl. I
(In A) I
Cl.
(in A) II
Solo
8va
rit.
Vl. I
Vl. II
Vla.
Vc.

a tempo
4
Solo
mp espress.
I.Solo
p
Solo
I. p
pp
I. senza sord.
mp
I. Solo
mp (sord.)
II.
p (open)
mp
a tempo
4
pp
pp
pp
I. Solo
mp espress.
I. Solo
mp espress.
HALF (div.)
p
p
p
p
p
Fl. I.
Ob. I. II
(in A) I
Cl.
(in A) II
Fg. I. II
Cor. (F) I. II
Tr. (B♭) I. II
Arpa
Vl. I
Vl. II
Vla.
Vc.

Ob. I. II
Fg. I. II
Cor. (F) I. II
Vl. I
Vl. II
Vla.
Vc.
I. Solo
p espress.
I.
p
HALF (unis.)
I. Solo
As at first
Solo
Allegro (♩ = 160)
Cl. I (in A)
Xylo.
Tabor (Long Dr.)
Pfte.
Arpa
Cb.
(cuivré)
sf
f
Vigoroso
8va
Tutti
pp
HALF

G.P.
I.
Fl.
II.
I. Solo
Ob. I. II
a 2
Solo
(in A) I
Cl.
(in A) II
I. Solo
Fg. I. II
Pfte.
Vl. I
Vl. II
HALF pizz.
Vla.
Tutti arco
Vc.

7
marc.
a 2
Ob. I. II
f
(in A) I
Cl.
(in A) II
f marc.
f marc.
Cor. (F) I. II
(cuivré)
(cuivré)
f
Xylo.
f
Tabor
sf
Pfte.
8va
f marc.
Vl. I
f marc.
Vl. II
f marc.
Vla.
f marc.
Vc.
pizz.
arco
p
Fl. I.
Fl. II.
Solo
mf
2 Soli div.
div. (½ arco pizz.)
sim.

8
non legato
I.
Fl.
II.
non legato
Ob.
I. II
non legato
(In A) I
f non legato
Cl.
(in A) II
f non legato
Cor. (F)
I. II
(Open) a 2
f marc.
Tr. (B♭)
I. II
(Open)
a 2
f marc.
Trb.
I. II
a 2
f marc.
8
8va
Pfte.
f non legato (bell like)
8
2 Soli
Tutti
div.
Vl. I
f marc.
unis.
arco
Vl. II
f marc.
unis.
arco
Vla.
f marc.
Vc.

Fl.
I.
II.
Ob. I. II
Cl.
(in A) I
(in A) II
Fg. I. II
Cor. (F) I. II
Tr. (B♭) I. II
Trb. I. II
Xylo.
Pfte.
Vl. I
Vl. II
Vla.
Vc.
Cb.
9
f
ff
a 2
8va
unis.
unis. arco
f marc.
Tutti

I.
Fl.
II.
Fg. I. II
a 2
Cor. (F) I. II
Tr. (B♭) I. II
Trb. I. II
Xylo.
Pfte.
8va
Vl. I
Vl. II
Vla.
Vc.
Cb.

I.
Fl.
II.
Ob. I. II
a 2
f
(in A) I
Cl.
(in A) II
Fg. I. II
a 2
Cor. (F) I. II
Tr. (B♭) I. II
Trb. I. II
8va
Pfte.
8
Vl. I
8va
Vl. II
Vla.
Vc.
Cb.

⑩
I.
Fl.
II.
a 2
Ob.
I. II
(in A) I
Cl.
(in A) II
a 2
Fg.
I. II
I.
Cor. (F)
I. II
Tr. (B♭)
I. II
Trb.
I. II
⑩
8va
Vl. I
Vl. II
Vla.
Vc.
Cb.

Fl. I
Ob. I. II
(in A) I
Cl.
(in A) II
Fg. I. II
Cor. (F) I. II
Tr. (Bb) I. II
Trb. I. II
Timp.
Tri.
Pfte.
Vl. I
Vl. II
Vla.
Vc. Cb.
Solo
mf
I. Solo
p
Solo
p
Solo
p
Solo
p
Solo
p
I. Solo
p
G. P.
11
Change to Bb
Change to Bb
a 2
sub. f marc.
G. P.
a 2
sub. f marc.
f
f secco
8
G. P.
11
f
pizz.
f
f
f

I.
Fl.
II.
Ob. I. II
(in B♭) I
Cl.
(in B♭) II
Fg. I. II
a 2
Cor. (F) I. II
a 2
Tr. (B♭) I. II
Timp.
Xylo.
Pfte.
Vl. I
Vl. II
arco
Vla.
Vc. Cb.
f marc.

Solo
I.
Fl.
II.
Ob.
I. II
(in B♭) I
Cl.
(in B♭) II
Cor. (F)
I. II
a 2
Tr. (B♭)
I. II
Timp.
Xylo.
ARPA
Pfte.
Vl. I
Vl. II
Vla.
Vc.

12
I.
Fl.
II.
non legato
non legato
Ob.
I. II
a 2
f
non legato
(in B♭) I
Cl.
(in B♭) II
Cor. (F)
I. II
f marc.
Tr. (B♭)
I. II
f
mf
Arpa
p
12
Vl. I
f marc.
Vl. II
f marc.
Vla.
f marc.
Vc.
f marc.
Cb.
f marc.

I.
Fl.
II.
Ob.
I. II
(in Bb) I
(in Bb) II
Fg.
I. II
Cor. (F)
I. II
Tr. (Bb)
I. II
Trb.
I. II
Tabor
Pfte.
Vl. I
Vl. II
Vla.
Vc.
Cb.
a 2
f
sf
I.

13
I.
Fl.
II.
a 2
Ob. I. II
(in B♭) I
Cl.
(in B♭) II
Fg. I. II
Cor. (F) I. II
Tr. (B♭) I. II
Trb. I. II
Tabor
Pfte.
Vl. I
Vl. II
Vla.
Vc.
Cb.
fff
ff
f
f cresc.
cresc.
8va

Solo
I.
Fl.
II.
Ob.
I.II
a 2
(in Bb) I
Cl.
(in Bb) II
Fg.
I.II
Cor. (F)
I.II
marc.
Tr. (Bb)
I.II
Trb.
I.II
Timp.
Xylo.
Tabor
8va
Pfte.
Vl. I
Vl. II
Vla.
div.
mf espress.
Vc.
Cb.
Vc.
Vc. e Cb.

14
Fl. I
14
Vl. I
mp
Vl. II
p
Vla.
unis.
p
Vc.
div.
mf
unis.
p
Cb.
mf
p
I.
Fl.
II.
15
Solo
pp
Glock.
pp
Arpa
pp
15
Vl. I
Vl. II
Vla.
Vc.
Cb.

I.
Fl.
II.
Solo
mp
G. P.
Solo
pp
Ob.
I. II
I. Solo
mp
I Solo
p
(in Bb) I
Cl.
(in Bb) II
Solo
p
pp
Fg.
I. II
II. Solo
mp
I. Solo
mp
16 Moderato (♩ = 104)
(♩ = ♪)
Twice as slow
17 (♩ = 52)
Solo
mf espress.
I.
II.
p
Cor. (F)
I. II
I. con sord.
p
Tr. (B)
I. II
I. con sord.
p
Trb.
I. II
I. con sord.
p
I.
Arpa
secco
p

a tempo primo (♪ = ♩)

(♩ = ♪) As before (a trifle slower (♩ = 50)

18

Ob. I. II — I. Solo — *mf* espress.

(in B♭) I Cl. (in B♭) II — *p*

Fg. I. II — *p*

Trb. I. II — I. — *p*

Arpa

a tempo primo (♪ = ♩)

(♩ = ♪) As before (a trifle slower (♩ = 50)

18

Vl. I — 4 Vlns. div. — *p*

Vl. II — 4 Vlns. div. — *p*

Vla. — 2 Vlas. — *p*

a tempo primo (♪ = ♩)

Slower (♩ = 80)

(in B♭) I Cl. (in B♭) II — *mp*

Fg. I. II — *p* — I.

Cor. (F) I. II — I. — *p* — senza sord.

Trb. I. II — I. — *p*

Arpa

19 Much slower, poco rubato (♩ = 69)
Press forward
Cl (in B♭) I
Cl (in B♭) II
Fg. I. II
Cor. (F) I. II
(cuivré)
Tutti
con sord.
f molto espress.
sim.
Vl. I
Vl. II
Vla.
Vc.
rit. - - - a tempo
Ob. I. II
(Open)
Tr. (B♭) I. II
meno f

20
Più accel.
rit.
a tempo
Poco accel.
(in B♭) I
Cl.
(in B♭) II
Fg. I. II
Cor. (F) I. II
Tr. (B♭) I. II
Vl. I
Vl. II
Vla.
Vc.
Cb
con sord.
Ob. I. II
a 2
21
Poco accel.
rit.
Cb.

Slower (𝅗𝅥 = 52)
Fl. I
Ob. I. II
I. Solo
p tenderly
mp
tenderly
(in B♭) I
Cl.
(in B♭) II
I. Solo
p tenderly
Fg. I. II
Slower (𝅗𝅥 = 52)
4 Vlns. div.
senza sord.
Vl. I
p
2 Vlns.
Vl. II
senza sord.
p
4 Vlas
div.
Vla.
p
senza sord.
4 Vlcs. div.
Vc.
p
senza sord.
22
As before (𝅗𝅥 = 63)
Fl. I
Solo
pp
Cl. II (in B♭)
(II.)
pp
Fg. I. II
I.
mp
p
Vl. I
Tutti
senza sord.
As before (𝅗𝅥 = 63)
ppp
Vl. II
Tutti
senza sord.
ppp
Vla.
Tutti. senza sord.
ppp
Vc.
Tutti. senza sord.
ppp

23 Fast (♩=132)
Fl.
I.
II.
Fl. II = Picc. I
PICC.
Solo
mp
Ob. I. II
Playfully
I. Solo
Cl. I (in B♭)
Tri.
p
Vl. I
Vl. II
Vla.
pizz.
fp
Fl. I
Picc.
(Picc.) Solo
mf

24
Fl. I
Ob. I. II
a 2
mf
Cl. I (in B♭)
Fg. I. II
I.
p
Cor. (F) I. II
I. con sord.
fp
Tr. (B♭) I. II
II. Solo
p
Wood Bl.
24
p
Vl. I
mf
Playfully
Vl. II
Vla.
fp
25
8va
Fl. I
mp
Picc.
PICC.
mp
Ob. I. II
a 2
Cl. I (in B♭)
mp
Fg. I. II
a 2
Soli
f
Tr. (B♭) I. II
II.
mf
Trb. I. II
senza sord.
I. non legato
f
Wood Bl. Tri.
Wood Bl.
Tri.
p
Vl. I
mf
pizz
mp
Vl. II
p
mf
mp
Vla.
f
Vc.
pizz.
f

Fl. I
Picc.
Ob. I. II
a 2
mf
Cl. (in B♭) I
Cl. (in B♭) II
mf
Fg. I. II
a 2
f
Cor. (F) I. II
I. non legato
f
II. con sord.
Trb. I. II
I.
Tri.
Vl. I
Vl. II
Vla.
f
Vc.
f
arco

Fl. I
Picc.
Ob. I.II
(in B♭) I
Cl.
(in B♭) II
Fg. I.II
Cor. (F) I.II
Tr. I.II
Snare Dr. Tri.
Vl. I
Vl. II
Vla.
a 2
mf
f
Change to Clar. in A
II. secco
senza sord.
(cuivrè)
I. Solo
Tri.
Sn. Drum Brush on
sf
p
div. secco
p secco
26
Ob. I.II
Cl. I (in A)
Fg. I.II
Tr. I.II.
Sn. Dr.
Vl. II
Vla.
II.
secco
mp
(Brush)

I.
Fl.
Picc.
mf
mf
Ob. I. II
I.
Solo
(in A) I
Cl.
(in A) II
mf
secco
p
Fg. I. II
mp
Sn.Dr.
Stick (on rim)
stacc.
Pfte.
mp
Vl. I
arco
mp
Vl. II
unis.
mp
Vla.
div.
mp

27
Fl. I.
Picc.
mp
Ob. I. II
a 2
mp
Cl. (in A) I.
Cl. (in A) II
mp
Fg. I. II
Cor. (F) I. II
I. con sord.
p
Tr. (B♭) I. II
con sord.
p
Trb. I. II
II. con sord.
p
Pfte.
p stacc.
Vl. I
Vl. II
div.
pizz.
p
Vla.
unis.
pizz.
p
Vc.
pizz.
p

28 More deliberate tempo (♩= 126)
Fl.
I.
Picc.
(Picc. = Fl. II.)
Ob. I. II
a 2
(in A) I
Cl.
(in A) II
Fg. I. II
Cor. (F) I. II
I.
Tr. (B♭) I. II
Trb. I. II
I. con sord.
II.
Timp.
Pfte.
28 More deliberate tempo (♩=126)
sf
28 More deliberate tempo (♩=126)
Vl. I
arco
heavy accents
Vl. II
arco
heavy accents
Vla.
arco
div.
heavy accents
Vc.
Cb.
pizz.

Vl. I
Vl. II
Vla.
(div.)
(in A) I
Cl.
(in A) II
Cor. (F) I. II
Tr. (B♭) I. II
Trb. I. II
Timp.
Sn. Dr.
Pfte.
Vc.
Cb.
29
mf non legato, relaxed
a 2 senza sord.
II. senza sord.
senza sord.
(on rim)
mp leggiero
unis.
arco
mp stacc.

a 2
Ob. I. II
(in A) I
Cl.
(in A) II
a 2
Cor. (F) I. II
I. senza sord.
Tr. (B♭) I. II
Trb. I. II
Timp.
Sn.Dr.
Pfte.
sim.
Vl. I
sim.
Vl. II
sim.
Vla.
Vc.
Cb.

Ob. I. II
a 2
(in A) I.
Cl.
(in A) II
Cor. (F) I. II
a 2
Tr. (B♭) I. II
f
Trb. I. II
Timp.
Sn. Dr.
2 Sticks
f
Pfte.
Vl. I
f marc.
div.
Vl. II
f marc.
Vla.
f marc.
Vc.
Cb

30
Ob. I. II
f
(in A) I.
Cl.
(in A) II
f
f
Fg. I. II
a 2
f
Cor. (F) I. II
Tr. (B♭) I. II
Trb. I. II
8va (ad lib.)
8va (ad lib)
Timp.
Sn. Dr.
30
Pfte.
f
30
Vl. I
Vl. II
Vla.
Vc.
f
Cb.
f

I.
Fl.
II.
Ob
I. II
a 2
(in A) I.
Cl.
(in A) II
8va
Fg.
I. II
ff marc.
Cor. (F)
I. II
marc.
Tr. (B♭)
I. II
ff marc.
Trb.
I. II
Timp.
Sn. Dr.
Pfte.
Vl. I
Vl. II
unis.
Vla.
Vc.
Cb.

8va
I.
Fl.
II.
a 2
Ob. I. II
(in A) I.
Cl.
(in A) II.
Fg. I. II
Cor. (F) I. II
Tr. (B♭) I. II
Trb. I. II
Pfte.
Vl. I
Vl. II
Vla.
Vc.
marc.
sfz

31
Ob. I. II
a 2
f
(in A) I.
Cl.
(in A) II.
f
f
Fg. I. II
a 2
f pesante
Cor. (F) I. II
a 2
f pesante
f
Tr. (B♭) I. II
Solo
II.
f
Trb. I. II
f pesante
Tabor
f pesante
Bass Dr.
mf pesante, secco
31
Pfte.
f pesante
31
Vl. I
Vl. II
pizz.
f
Vla.
pizz.
f
Vc.
pizz.
f
Cb.
sim.
f pesante e ritmico

Ob. I. II
a 2
(in A) I.
Cl.
(in A) II
8va
Fg. I. II
a 2
Cor. (F) I. II
a 2
Tr. (B♭) I. II
Trb. I. II
Timp.
f pesante
Tabor
32
Pfte.
f pesante
Vl. I
f
Vl. II
arco
f
Vla.
div.
unis.
arco
f pesante
Vc.
arco
f pesante
Cb.
f

8va
I.
Fl.
II.
ff marc.
Ob. I. II
a 2
(in A) I
Cl.
(in A) II
Fg. I. II
Cor. (F) I. II
Tr. (B♭) I. II
ff
Trb. I. II
Timp.
Tri. Cym.
Tri.
f
susp. Cym. (hard stick)
Pfte.
Vl. I
Vl. II
div.
Vla.
Vc.
Cb

33
Molto Moderato (♩ = 66)
I.
Fl.
II.
Ob.
I. II
(in A) I.
Cl.
(in A) II
Fg.
I. II
a 2
fff
ff
Cor. (F)
I. II
(a 2)
Tr. (B♭)
I. II
Trb.
I. II
Timp.
Tri.
Cym.
Vl. I
8va
eloquent ff
Vl. II
unis.
Vla.
Vc.
unis
Cb.

Meno mosso 34
Fl.
I.
II.
Ob. I. II
Cl (in A) I.
(in A) II
Solo
Fg. I. II
II.
I. Solo
Cor. (F) I. II
a 2
Tr. (B♭) I. II
Trb. I. II
Meno mosso 34
Vl. I
Vl. II
Vla.
Vc.
Cb.
HALF
HALF (div.)
mf
p
f

Meno mosso
ancora
Solo
rit.
35
sub. Allegro
pp
p espress.
Fl. II = Picc.
PICC.
mp
I. Solo
mp espress.
I.
Change to
Clarinets in B♭
Claves
mf
8va
Meno mosso
ancora
rit.
35
sub. Allegro
sub. Allegro
Meno mosso
ancora
HALF (div.)
rit.
Tutti, non div.
At the frog.
sfz
Tutti
unis
Tutti
Fl.
I.
II.
Ob.
I. II
(in A) I
Cl.
(in A) II
Fg.
I. II
Arpa
Pfte.
Vl. I
Vl. II
Vla.
Vc.
Cb.

Fl. I
Picc.
Ob. I. II
(in B♭) I.
Cl.
(in B♭) II
Fg. I. II
Tr. (B♭) I. II
Trb. I. II
Claves
Arpa
Pfte.
Vl. I
Vl. II
Vla.
Vc.
36
a 2
8va
mp
mf
sf

Cor. (F) I. II
Tr. (B♭) I. II
Trb. I. II
Vl. I
Vl. II
Vla.
Vc.
Cb.
ff
mf
sfz
sf
p
Accel.
37 Presto (𝅗𝅥 = 92) 8va
Fl. I. II.
Fg. I. II
mp
non legato
mp stacc.

Fl. I
Cl. II (in B♭)
Fg. I. II
I.
II.
p
non legato
mp
Vl. I
Vl. II
Vla.
p stacc.
8va
38
Fl. I
Picc.
Ob. I. II
Soli
a 2
(in B♭) I.
Cl.
(in B♭) II.
Fg. I. II
sf
sfz
mp
Cor. (F) I. II
con sord.
Tr. (B♭) I. II
con sord
Vl. I
Vl. II
Vla.
Vc.
pizz.
mf
non div.

sim.
a 2
Ob. I. II
(in B♭) I.
Cl.
(in B♭) II
Fg. I. II
mf
f
ff
p
Cor. (F) I. II
senza sord.
Tr. (B♭) I. II
39
Vl. I
arco
mp
Vl. II
(pizz.)
Vla.
Vc.
Cb.
pizz.
I.
con sord.
non legato
arco

40
I.
Fl.
Picc.
f marc.
sf
f
Ob. I. II
p non legato
(in B♭) I.
Cl.
(in B♭) II
Fg. I. II
Cor. (F) I. II
con sord.
Tr. (B♭) I. II
Trb. I. II
Vl. I
Vl. II
Vla.
Vc.

I.
Fl.
Picc.
Ob.
I. II
a 2
(in B♭) I.
Cl.
(in B♭) II.
Cor. (F)
I. II
a 2
Tr. (B♭)
I. II
Trb.
I. II
Timp.
Bass Dr.
Pfte.
stacc.
8va
41
Vl. I
div.
marc.
Vl. II
Vla.
Vc.
Cb
arco

8va
Fl.
I.
Picc.
Ob. I. II
Cl.
(in B♭) I
(in B♭) II
a 2
Cor. (F) I. II
Tr. (B♭) I. II
Trb. I. II
Timp.
B. Dr.
unis.
Vl. I
unis.
Vl. II
Vla.
Vc.
Cb.

42
8va
I. Fl.
Picc.
Ob. I. II
(in B♭) I Cl. (in B♭) II
Cor. (F) I. II
a 2
Tr. (B♭) I. II
Trb. I. II
Timp.
B. Dr.
Vl. I
Vl. II
Vla.
Vc.
Cb.
cresc.
ff
mf
mp
At the frog
Mark the Bass

8va
I.
Fl.
Picc.
Fg.
I. II
a 2
Cor. (F)
I. II
Vl. I
Vl. II
Vla.
Vc.
Cb.
8

43
I.
Fl.
Picc.
Ob. I. II
(in B♭) I.
Cl.
(in B♭) II.
Fg. I. II
a 2
Cor. (F) I. II
senza sord.
Tr. (B♭) I. II
Trb. I. II
Claves
Arpa
Pfte.
Vl. I
Vl. II
Vla.
Vc.
Cb.
mf
f
sf
8va

44
Vl. I
Vl. II
Vla.
Vc.
Cb.
mf
a 2
Ob. I. II
f marc.
(in B♭) I.
Cl.
(in B♭) II.
Fg. I. II
Cor. (F) I. II
Tr. (B♭) I. II
f
mf
Pfte.
mf non legato
div.
f marc.

45
I.
Fl.
Picc.
Ob. I. II
(in B♭) I
Cl.
(in B♭) II
Fg. I. II
Cor. (F) I. II
Tr. (B♭) I. II
Trb. I. II
Pfte.
Vl. I
Vl. II
Vla.
Vc.
Cb.
Solo
a 2
unis.
div.
pizz.

46
I.
Fl.
Picc.
8va
Take Fl. II.
Pres de la table
Arpa
p
46
div.
pizz.
arco
unis.
Vl. I
p
arco
Vl. II
Vla.
Fl. I
Fg. I. II
I.
Tr. (B♭) I. II
I.II con sord.
p
Arpa
Vl. I
Vl. II
unis.
Vla.

47
I.
Fl.
II.
mf
mf
a 2
Ob. I. II
sf-mf
sf
mf
(in Bb) I
Cl.
(in Bb) II
sf-mf
sf
Fg. I. II
Tr. (Bb) I. II
sf-p
unis.
Vl. I
Vl. II
Vla.
Vc.
Cb.
p

I.
Fl.
II.
Ob.
I. II
(in B♭) I
Cl.
(in B♭) II
Fg.
I. II
Cor. (F)
I. II
II. (senza sord.)
I. senza sord.
Tr. (B♭)
I. II
div.
pizz.
unis.
Vl. I
pizz.
Vl. II
Vla.
Vc.
mf
f
ff
p
mp

48
I.
Fl.
II.
Ob. I.II
(in B♭) I
Cl.
(in B♭) II
Fg. I.II
Cor. (F) I.II
Tr. (B♭) I.II
Trb. I.II
Xylo.
Pfte.
Vl. I
Vl. II
Vla.
Vc.
secco
a 2
arco
f marc.
cresc.
mf
p
f
ff
8va

I.
Fl.
II.
8va
Ob.
I. II
a 2
(in Bb) I
Cl.
(in Bb) II
Fg.
I. II
Cor. (F)
I. II
Tr. (Bb)
I. II
Trb.
I. II
Xylo.
8
Pfte.
Vl. I
Vl. II
Vla.
Vc.

49
I.
Fl.
II.
Ob.
I. II
(in Bb) I
Cl.
(in Bb) II
Fg.
I. II
a 2
Cor. (F)
I. II
Tr. (Bb)
I. II
Trb.
I. II
Timp.
Xylo.
Pfte.
Vl. I
Vl. II
Vla.
Vc.
Cb.
sf
ff
ff marc.
8va
div.
unis.
marc.
II.

I.
Fl.
II.
Ob. I. II
(in B♭) I
Cl.
(in B♭) II
a 2
Fg. I. II
Cor. (F) I. II
Tr. (B♭) I. II
Trb. I. II
Timp.
Xylo.
Claves
Arpa
Pfte
Vl. I
Vl. II
Vla.
Vc.
Cb.
sf
ff
unis.
div.
8va

More deliberate tempo (𝅗𝅥 = 120)
50
I.
Fl.
II.
Ob. I. II
(in B♭) I.
Cl.
(in B♭) II.
Fg. I. II
Cor. (F) I. II
Tr. (B♭) I. II
Trb. I. II
Xylo. Timp.
Claves
Arpa
Pfte.
Vl. I
Vl. II
Vla.
Vc.
Cb.
a 2
ten.
unis.
Xyl.
Timp.
8va
pizz.
sf
f

rit.
Meno mosso (♩ = 96)
51
ten.
I.
Fl.
II.
a 2
Ob.
I. II
I. Solo
sub. mf cant. espress.
(in B♭) I.
Cl.
(in B♭) II
Fg.
I. II
Cor. (F)
I. II
Tr. (B♭)
I. II
Trb.
I. II
Timp.
sf
Arpa
mf (brittle)
8va
Vl. Solo
cant.
sub. mf 51 dolce
Vl. I
p dolce
Vl. II
Vla.
Vc.
dolce
Cb.
arco
pizz.
(pizz.)
p

Fl. I
Ob. I. II
Cl. I (in B♭)
Fg. I. II
Arpa
Vl. Solo
Vl. I
Vl. II
Vla.
Vc.
Cb.
52
I.
Solo
p cant.
8va
div.
arco
pizz.
p
pp
ppp

As at first (slowly)
53
Fl. I.
(in B♭) I.
Cl.
(in B♭) II
Fg. I. II
Solo
I. Solo
Tr. (B♭) I. II
I. Solo
con sord.
Arpa
As at first (slowly)
53
Vl. II
Vla.
Vc.
div.
div.
54
Fl. I.
Solo
Cl. II
Fg. I. II
I.
Tr (B♭) I. II
I.
Arpa
54
Vl. I
unis.
Vl. II
unis.
div.
Vla.
unis.
Vc. Cb.
unis Vc.
Vc., Cb.

* Shaker melody "The gift to be simple"

57
A trifle faster (♩= 80)
Fl. I
Picc.
Take Fl. II
Ob. I. II
II.
I. Solo
(in B♭) I.
Cl.
(in B♭) II
Solo
Fg. I. II
II. Solo
Tr. (B♭) I. II
con sord.
Arpa
58
I.
Fl.
II.
Ob. I. II
a 2
Fg. I. II
Cor. (F) I. II
(Open)
Tr. (B♭) I. II
Tri.

I.
Fl.
II.
(a 2)
I. Solo
Ob.
I. II
mf
(in B♭) I
Cl.
(in B♭) II
Solo
Fg.
I. II
II.
Cor. (F)
I. II
Glock.
sounds 8va
p
8va
Arpa
Pfte.
senza Ped.
Vl. I
div.
pizz.
Vl. II

59
I.
Fl.
II.
p leggiero
Ob.
I. II
(in B♭) I
Cl.
(in B♭) II
Fg.
I. II
con sord.
Cor. (F)
I. II
p
I. Solo cant.
Trb.
I. II
mf dolce
Glock.
sounds 8va
8va
Arpa
Pfte.
Vl. I
Vl. II
Vla.
mf cant. dolce

60
I.
Fl.
II.
Ob.
I. II
(in B♭) I
Cl.
(in B♭) II
Fg.
I. II
Cor. (F)
I. II
senza sord.
a 2
f cant.
Tr. (B♭)
I. II
senza sord.
mf
Trb.
I. II
I.
a 2
Glock.
sounds 8va
8va
Arpa
8va
Pfte.
Vl. I
cant. sonore
div.
60
f
Vl. II
Vla.
Vc.
Cb.
f sonore

I.
Fl.
II.
Ob.
I.II
(in B♭) I
Cl.
(in B♭) II
Fg.
I.II
a 2
Cor. (F)
I.II
Tr. (B♭)
I.II
a 2
Trb.
I.II
Glock.
sounds 8va
8va
Arpa
8va
Pfte.
Vl. I
Vl. II
Vla.
Vc.
Cb.

I.
Fl.
II.
Ob.
I. II
(in B♭) I
Cl.
(in B♭) II
Fg.
I. II
a 2
Cor. (F)
I. II
Tr. (B♭)
I. II
a 2
Trb.
I. II
Glock.
sounds 8va
8va
Arpa
8va
Pfte.
Vl. I
Vl. II
Vla.
Vc.
Cb.

Solo
61
I.
Fl.
II.
Ob.
I. II
I. Solo
p
(in B♭) I
Cl.
(in B♭) II
Solo
Fg.
I. II
Cor. (F)
I. II
a 2
Tr. (B♭)
I. II
Trb.
I. II
Glock.
sounds 8va
8va
Arpa
Pfte.
Vl. I
Vl. II
arco
p sostenuto
Vla.
Vc.
Cb.
pizz.

move forward
(♪=♩)
62 Doppio movimento
Fl. I
Ob. I. II
(in B♭) I
Cl.
(in B♭) II
Fg. I. II
mf cresc.
non legato
Cor. (F) I. II
mf cresc.
Tr. (B♭) I. II
Vigoroso e marc.
a 2
Trb. I. II
II.
mf cresc. f
move forward
62 Doppio movimento
div.
Vl. I
mf cresc.
Vl. II
f cresc.
Vla.
mf cresc.
Vc.
mf cresc.
Tr. (B♭) I. II
a 2
Trb. I. II
unis.
Vl. I
f
Vla.
f

63
Ob. I. II
a 2
f sf Vigoroso e marc.
(in B♭) I
Cl.
(in B♭) II
f sf Vigoroso e marc.
f sf Vigoroso e marc.
Cor. (F) I. II
a 2 sf
Tr. (B♭) I. II
a 2
sf
Trb. I. II
a 2 sf
Ob. I. II
a 2
(in B♭) I
Cl.
(in B♭) II
Cor. (F) I. II
a 2
Tr. (B♭) I. II
a 2
Trb. I. II
a 2
Vl. I
Vla.

64 A trifle slower (𝅗𝅥 = 66)
Ob. I. II
I. Solo
mf
Cl. (in B♭) I
Solo
mf
Cl. (in B♭) II
mf
Fg. I. II
I. Solo
mf
Tr. (B♭) I. II
a 2
p
Trb. I. II
a 2
p
64 A trifle slower (𝅗𝅥 = 66)
Vl. I
Vla.
Vc. Cb.
arco
p
Fl. I.
Fl. II.
mf
mf
Ob. I. II
I.
Cl. (in B♭) I
Cl. (in B♭) II
Fg. I. II
I.
Vc. Cb.

(𝅗𝅥 = 𝅗𝅥) Broadly (in 2)
65
Fl.
I.
II.
fff legato e marc.
Ob. I. II
a 2
Cl.
(in B♭) I.
(in B♭) II
marc.
Fg. I. II
Cor. (F) I. II
Tr. (B♭) I. II
Trb. I. II
Timp.
Arpa
Pfte.
8va
unis.
Vl. I
Vl. II
Vla.
Vc.
Cb.
fff marc.

66
67
(𝅗𝅥 = ♩) Moderato (♩ = 66)
Fl. I. II.
a 2
Ob. I. II
(in B♭) I Cl. (in B♭) II
Fg. I. II
Cor. (F) I. II
Tr. (B♭) I. II
Trb. I. II
Timp.
Arpa
Pfte.
8va
Vl. I
Like a prayer
con sord.
Vl. II
Vla.
Vc.
Cb.
sf
p
pp
ppp

poco rit.
68
a tempo
Vl. I
Vl. II
Vla.
Vc.
poco rit.
Vl. I
Vl. II
Vla.
Vc.
Cb.
con sord.
pp
69
Più mosso (♩ = 80)
I.
Fl.
II.
p dolce
p dolce
Ob.
I. II
I.
p dolce
(in B♭) I
Cl.
(in B♭) II
p dolce
p dolce
Fg.
I. II
I.
p dolce

70 a tempo (♩ = 66)
rit.
Andante (very calm) 𝅗𝅥 = 54
71
Solo
p sost. molto
I.
Fl.
II.
p
Ob. I. II
mf
(in B♭) I
Cl.
(in B♭) II
Fg. I. II
Cor. (F) I. II
I. con sord.
Vl. I
mf sonore
pp
Vl. II
Vla.
Vc.
Cb.

Fl. I.
Cl. I (in B♭)
Solo
p sost.
Arpa
p sost. molto
8va
Vl. Solo
Solo
p
HALF
Vl. I
p sost. molto
Vl. II
Vla.
Vc. Cb.
72
73
Glock.
pp
p ("white" tone)
laissez vibrer
Flag.
div.
Vc.
Cb